DATE DUE

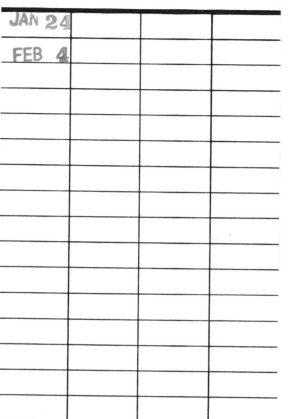

JAN 24			
FEB 4			

Plan B

Plan B

ONE MAN'S JOURNEY FROM TRAGEDY TO TRIUMPH

MIKE HARCOURT & JOHN LEKICH

John Wiley & Sons Canada, Ltd.

John Wiley & Sons Canada, Ltd.
6045 Freemont Boulevard, Mississauga, ON L5R 4J3

National Library of Canada Cataloguing in Publication

Harcourt, Michael, 1943-
    Plan B : one man's journey from tragedy to triumph / Mike Harcourt,
John Lekich.

Includes index.
ISBN 0-470-83504-4

    1. Harcourt, Michael, 1943-. 2. Accident victims—British
Columbia—Biography. 3. Prime ministers—British Columbia—Biography.
4. Politicians—British Columbia—Biography. I. Lekich, John II. Title.

FC3829.1.H37A3 2004   971.1'04'092   C2004-905294-2

Production Credits:
Cover: Sputnik Design Partners Inc.
Interior text design: Natalia Burobina
Author photos, front cover and back flap: Alex Waterhouse-Hayward
Printer: Tri-Graphic Printing Limited

Printed in Canada

10 9 8 7 6 5 4 3 2 1

CONTENTS

FOREWORD

In November 2002, I turned on the news to discover that Mike Harcourt had suffered a near-fatal fall off the deck of his North Pender Island cottage. He and his wife Beckie have been friends of my family's for years. So the news of his severe injury came as a great shock. Before the accident, Mike had been in great shape. As he approached sixty, his remarkable appetite for life seemed keener than ever. For the Harcourts, this was supposed to be a time of joy, relaxation, and a renewed commitment to the social issues that have always formed such an integral part of their lives. But fate had other plans.

In the hours following Mike's accident, things looked especially grim. Having been born with cerebral palsy, I know what it's like when your body refuses to do what you want it to. I realized that for Mike the future would include any number of seemingly impossible challenges. I consoled myself with a single positive thought: Mike Harcourt had always been a fighter. His sense of optimism and fair play is complemented by a relentless drive to meet his personal goals. Many people may be surprised to learn just how tough he really is.

I visited Mike shortly after the accident. At that time, nobody knew if he'd ever walk again. I remember thinking that I would have to do my best to try to cheer him up. Typically, his upbeat nature made me feel better. "It's time for Plan B, John," he said with a smile, letting me in on the first of many goals. "I'm bustin' out of this place."

As it turned out, both Mike and I would have experiences with Vancouver's G. F. Strong Rehabilitation Centre at different times in our lives. In fact, one of Mike's favourite stories involves my time there when I was still in preschool. Twice a year, I would be evaluated by a group of stern-looking doctors, who would ask me to walk down a long hallway in my underwear. Often, they requested that I walk as fast as I could. I would begin the long, barefoot journey toward my mother's arms. Walking, falling, getting up, and starting again—until I eventually arrived at the end of the hall. It's not surprising that Mike likes to tell this story. His favourite direction is forward. In fact, moving forward is what this book is all about. Both in terms of Mike's personal life and his public life, which encompasses the many social issues he has been devoted to for so many years. The goal? To provide hope and inspiration to people struggling with their own version of

Plan B. Just as Mike has been inspired by the countless personal stories he's encountered during the rehabilitation process.

As co-author of this work, I'm indebted to many dedicated health professionals who shared their own experiences with Mike. I thank them. I would also like to thank the writers who have followed Mike's continuing story. I am especially grateful to Lori Culbert's fine series in the *Vancouver Sun* and Wayne Skene, Mike's writing partner in *A Measure of Defiance*.

My deepest thanks go to Mike, Beckie, and their son Justen for opening their hearts and sharing so many private thoughts with me. They give new meaning to one of their favourite sayings, a remark made by Tommy Douglas: "What we wish for ourselves, we wish for others."

—John Lekich

five years of cottage life. They pulled up a basketful of beets and carrots from their back garden, then decided to clean the leaves from the eavestroughs. The couple went their separate ways when Mike had one more small task to carry out on the deck.

For no particular reason, Beckie changed her mind about waiting for Mike to rejoin her in their gardening chores. She went looking for him instead. The first place she headed for was the deck, a platform without a railing that stretched out from the living room and jutted to within fifteen feet of a rock cliff above the sea. But her husband wasn't on it. What was there instead sent a shiver up her neck. A stray bucket lay adrift on the damp wood, and one of the black leather carpet slippers Mike had been wearing was lying nearby at an odd angle.

∽∾∾

North Pender Island isn't the kind of place where you expect bad things to happen. It's the kind of destination you choose to put a suitable distance between yourself and the cares of the outside world. Joined to its sister South Pender Island by a bridge, the North Pender property comprises a hundred acres of farmland, forest, and recreational property The Harcourts are one of ten families who own the property. The view includes not only the ocean but a wide variety of trees, from Douglas firs to cedars. Every angle seemingly tailor-made for a postcard shot of the good life. It's the perfect spot for shorts and T-shirts, goofy snapshots on the beach, and forgetting to lock the door of your cabin.

2

ACKNOWLEDGEMENTS

Births, marriages, deaths—particularly the near-death experience I faced after falling from a twenty-foot cliff in front of my North Pender Island home—alter your perspective on life with a unique intensity. I hope this book, crafted by my talented co-writer, John Lekich, will show you how touched I was by the many inspirational people who helped me to get on with Plan B. These people include rescue workers, doctors, nurses, and therapists. But I was especially moved by the other people I met who live with the trauma of spinal cord injury—most of them far more seriously damaged than me.

My thanks go to my literary agent, Carolyn Swayze, and to John Wiley & Sons for believing in this book. The whole Wiley team—from executive editor Karen Milner to those in the editorial and publicity departments who worked on the project—made the entire experience both challenging and enjoyable.

I would also like to thank my guardian angel Beckie—my wife and the mother of our wonderful son Justen. It's only because of Beckie that I'm still here to get on with Plan B.

—Mike Harcourt

XI

1

A LIFE WORTH FIGHTING FOR

"I just basically said to myself, 'Hell, no. I'm not going to go this way.'"
— MIKE HARCOURT

It had started out as the kind of Gulf Island weekend that Mike and Beckie Harcourt had dreamed about for years. With the pressure of full-time politics firmly behind him and the teaching rollercoaster halted for her, the couple could now take full advantage of their oceanfront cottage on North Pender Island. Mike had traded in a shirt and tie for his usual island attire of jeans and a sweatshirt. It was November 30, but here in the middle of the Strait of Georgia, a minimum two-hour ferry ride away from Vancouver, city life was forgotten and the odd eagle was out gliding on the soft breeze.

After a leisurely lunch, Beckie and Mike began to do the chores that were typical of the season. The same tasks they had routinely performed for the last twenty-

In fact, the people who spend time there—from writers and artists to retired physicians and judges—never use the word *island* if they can help it. To them, it's just Pender. Maybe because, once you get to know the rhythm of the place, it's not really an island at all. It's more like a state of mind surrounded by water.

The surroundings have a way of encouraging helpful conversations with strangers. They may not know you on Pender, but if you're walking on the side of the road, people will wave from passing cars anyway. Often, someone will roll down their window and offer you a lift. Just in case you happen to have lost your way to a friend's place. Hitch a ride and you'll find that person always know who your friend is and the quickest way to get to that waterfront view on their deck.

There's an unwritten code about lending a helping hand that residents of such places immediately understand. A stranger to Pender once expressed surprise when he chanced to observe Mike Harcourt and a few other veterans of the island attempting to push a neighbour's car out of the ditch. Mike was premier of British Columbia at the time and—as the observer noticed—he seemed to be pushing at least as hard as everybody else. There were no cameras to turn the moment into a folksy piece of political propaganda. No spin doctors to point out the obvious—that this was a decent gesture from a typically decent man. It was just a few guys trying to help a friend.

There are more than a few well-known and successful people who have places on Pender, but Mike Harcourt is probably the most recognizable. Thanks to a popular three-term run as mayor of Vancouver—where he developed an impressive track record of social entrepreneurship that paved a clear road to the premier's office—he would inevitably become something of a local institution, as much a part of what made the city unique as White Spot burgers, the Woodward's *W*, or the sound of the Nine o'Clock gun.

Describing himself as a fiscally conservative social democrat, Mike Harcourt displays a sensible mix of empathy and responsibility that would strike a positive chord with British Columbia's voters. His three rules for running a successful business ("Treat your workers fairly, don't mess up the environment, and pay your fair share of taxes.") also say a great deal about his straight-shooting style of governing. It was a style many people could relate to.

After winning a seat on Vancouver's city council in 1972, Mike would hold some form of office for most of the next twenty-five years. As veteran correspondent Johnny Apple acknowledged in the *New York Times*, Mike's decades of work as "an apostle for transit, green zones and wilderness reserves," is a fundamental reason that today's Vancouver is consistently rated one of the world's most livable cities.

In an interview, he told Apple that Vancouver's biggest challenge for the foreseeable future was how to prepare for the city's inevitable growth while preserving its soul. "Everyone wants to live here," he said, when asked about the increasing number of people settling in Vancouver from all over the world. Few

Vancouverites were better equipped to understand the reasons that so many others want to move to the place or, for that matter, what makes up its soul. Mike Harcourt lived in Vancouver's affluent Kerrisdale as a boy—experiencing a childhood he describes as idyllic—and his abiding loyalty would inevitably spread to every corner of the city. He would cherish what worked and try to change what didn't. But, most importantly, he would always understand what made it unique.

The roots of his activism can be traced to a single desire. He wanted to stop Vancouver from becoming a misguided echo of Los Angeles in the name of runaway commerce, the kind of city where urban sprawl stops at the water simply because there's no place left to expand. He knew the appeal of Vancouver resided in the sheer welcome of its livability. And he wanted others to share in that welcome, just as he had.

∾∾∾

When Mike and Beckie cleaned the wet leaves out of the Pender cottage eavestroughs on that November day in 2002, spillage left the surface of the deck a little slippery, but it wasn't an immediate concern. Mike, alone on the deck for just one more routine task, didn't think twice about it. His final task was to top off the hot tub with hot water. Mike and Beckie had added the generous hot tub—one of the cottage's true luxuries—in 2000. It sat just outside the master bedroom and was often in use. Mike had performed the simple chore of topping the tub off with water many times. For him, this was almost second nature.

The last thing Mike remembers clearly was filling up a couple of buckets in the kitchen and—with a full bucket in each hand—walking toward the hot tub. In that moment, there was nothing to suggest what would follow.

⌒⌒

Asked why he got into politics, Mike once said that all he wanted to do was make a difference for people who don't have money, power, or privilege.

He was born in Edmonton, Alberta, but moved to British Columbia with his family in time to enter kindergarten. Due to his dad's work, Mike moved a number of times during his childhood. By his early teens, he had attended nine schools in Vancouver and Victoria. He learned many things in the process. Among them: how to make friends fast, how to appreciate his immediate surroundings, and—perhaps most important of all—how to listen to different points of view from a variety of people.

One of his earliest acts as mayor was to initiate a monthly Citizen's Day, an unprecedented feature of city hall where anyone could air a civic grievance as long as they booked an appointment. He wanted to make sure that people had a consistent forum for their concerns.

Complaints ranged from topics such as barking dogs to the disposal of leaves in the fall. He recalls that a woman came in wearing tinfoil around her head, claiming that her neighbour was pelting her with death rays. He was able to convince her that it was safe to remove the tinfoil because the engineering department had constructed an invisible shield of protection around her house.

Mike has said that his main reason for entering provincial politics was his commitment to settling treaties with the aboriginal people. The issues closest to his heart—including sustainable cities, the environment, disability issues, and aboriginal rights—have all benefited from an approach that's profoundly human. As leader of the opposition for BC's New Democratic Party, the first thing he did was visit every corner of the province.

"I genuinely like people," he has remarked, when asked about the personal satisfaction of tackling social problems through elected office.

His basic goals were the same through a political journey that has covered nine elections. Along the way, there was always the sense that he had a lot in common with the average citizen. A T-shirt logo for one of his campaigns reduced him to his three most prominent features: a bald head, oversized glasses, and a moustache. As mayor, he shrugged off the perk of a chauffeur, preferring to drive his own car. You were more likely to see him jogging around the Stanley Park seawall than wearing the chain of office during some stuffy ceremony.

He would ultimately become such an integral part of Vancouver's culture that a local sculptor created a likeness of him that was eventually used in the city's centennial celebration in 1986. Shunning the usual cold, stately tribute in bronze, it was constructed from chicken wire, plaster, and wood. Lumpy, lifelike, and comfortably approachable, Mike's statue was clad in the kind of jogging suit you often see behind a shopping cart in the margarine aisle at Safeway. It was a tribute that could only come from the heart.

Mike Harcourt was never the sort of public figure who was all teeth and hair attached to an afterthought of a body. Watching him on TV, hunched over a microphone at some press conference, you always had the sense that he was a big man obliged to accommodate a much smaller world. Journalists typically made the most of his appearance. While editorial cartoons had a way of conveniently shrinking him to the size of a middle-aged Charlie Brown, columnist Allan Fotheringham wrote that he looked like "a small town pharmacist."

Over the years, Mike has used the subject of his TV image to express his view that the true measure of a human being has little to do with the world of tight camera angles and even tighter editing. Ironically, a couple of favourite Harcourtisms cut to the chase of what he's about with the succinctness of a perfect sound bite. "If you want entertainment, get a video," he has said. And, "What you see is what you get."

With Mike, what you get beyond the confines of a talking box is taller than you might expect. At six feet three inches, his height has allowed him to indulge a lifelong passion for basketball. He was the star of his high-school team and later proved good enough to shoot hoops for the University of British Columbia on a combined academic and athletic scholarship. *Vancouver Sun* sportswriter Gary Mason named Mike the best player in a weekly pick-up basketball game consisting of various reporters and politicians.

Old friends have long known Mike as an avid tennis player and golfer. He believes in living comfortably while rejecting many of the ostentatious trappings that distinguish the most successful of his generation. The trunk of his aging Volvo has enough room for a rare indulgence—a set of custom-made clubs that accommodates his long reach. His wife, Beckie, has called him "the best skier of his age I've ever seen on the slopes of Whistler."

During his days in political office, his gait possessed a certain ambling grace that the television screen could never capture. As a kid, he played everything from soccer to little league baseball. Sports, he says, have always been a huge part of his life, and they have given him a sense of physical ease.

He's always been equally comfortable with the generous scope of his personal philosophy. "I've never looked at why you can't do something," he says. "Some people think of me as disgustingly optimistic. But why shouldn't I be? Just about everything I've set out to do or be has succeeded far beyond my initial expectations. In many ways, I've led a charmed life."

Maybe that's why Mike Harcourt and North Pender Island have always been such a perfect fit. It seems a charmed place.

༄

Even in November—traditionally BC's harshest month —there's something doggedly optimistic about the Pender setting. Torrents of rain can beat down from an endless blanket of grey sky. But this only seems to make the surroundings try harder to keep your attention. The trees turn a deeper green and the rocks on the nearby cliffs often glimmer with a wet sheen. At these times, it's not hard to believe that even the worst of storms will eventually pass.

You can fall in love with such a place. And that's exactly what happened to Mike and Beckie Harcourt when, as a young married couple, they decided to scrape up enough money to purchase a piece of waterfront property in 1973.

A couple of years later, they built a cottage on the site. In 1998—with an eye on turning the place into a second home—the cottage was expanded to two thousand square feet. Painted in subdued tones inspired by the natural environment, it has been remodelled into a luxurious haven that features everything from a state of the art kitchen to a dining room, where friends and guests are entertained. One of the Harcourts' favourite touches includes the generous windows that offer a spectacular view of Navy Channel.

To this day, Mike still can't get over the view from the deck, which he likens to a Toni Onley painting. We're kind of centred right in the heart of the Gulf Islands," he says. "We can see Galiano, Salt Spring. We can even see Mount Baker peering up over Mayne Island. It's just a magical place with all kinds of birds and wildlife right outside your window."

As the years passed, the view offered other pleasures as well. Mike and Beckie's son, Justen, spent his school holidays on Pender, growing up to explore every corner of the island. "When Justen was a little guy, he'd camp out on the beach with his friends," recalls Mike. "They'd build forts, roast marshmallows, and ride their bikes through the forest. He's always loved it there."

As Mike tells it, his family's time on the island was meaningful from the beginning. "It's always been a sanctuary and a place to feel peaceful and get your mind centred," he explains. "Maybe it's because you're so close to nature, but the ideas just flow."

"It's a very creative place," he continues. "There's just a lovely energy. I do a lot of my writing there. And Beckie has the garden. You can feel a sense of renewal, of reconnecting with something. As a family, it's been good for all three of us."

⚭

Three decades after the Harcourts purchased their place on Pender, it's difficult to conceive that Mike didn't initially set out to become a husband and father. While carving out a career as a storefront lawyer in the late 1960s—complete with a Fu-Manchu moustache and a commitment to social justice issues that would easily outlast a funky set of mutton chops—marriage was the last thing on his mind. "I figured that I was going to lead a high-risk existence working with the poor and disadvantaged," he explains. "A wife and family just didn't seem to fit in with that kind of life."

All that began to change when Mike first saw Beckie Salo from across the proverbial crowded room at a friend's house party. It was like a scene from the kind of romantic comedy they used to make in the seventies. Everybody happily packed in like sardines— laughing, drinking, and talking about things that matter. Zoom in on the young, streetwise lawyer who sees a stunning blonde with the kind of smile you can't help but notice from a distance. The movies would have cast Gene Hackman and Faye Dunaway, no doubt emphasizing their differences before they drifted apart in that vague, new Hollywood kind of way.

The reality proved somewhat different. For Mike, that initial glimpse of Beckie was not only a case of love at first sight but the beginning of a relationship that has lasted more than thirty years. Not that there weren't a few hurdles that would have delighted the average screenwriter. For starters, Mike had seen Beckie, but Beckie hadn't seen Mike. In fact, she'd left the party before he could get a chance to introduce himself.

Another kind of guy would have just gone to the fridge for a beer and waited for the moment to pass. Not Mike. He's always felt that there are times when you need to take a chance. Clearly, this was one of them. "I just had to do it," he remembers. After getting

Beckie's phone number from their mutual friend Janice Stewart, he made the call. "It was," he says, "the best decision of my life."

The plan was to ask Beckie to come along on a date with another couple. The evening would involve driving to Seattle to see a production of the musical *Hair*. Mike figured the drive would give him a chance to get to know Beckie. The trouble was his prospective date didn't have a clear idea of who he was. Plus, she'd already seen *Hair* twice. "I suggested that he take somebody else," Beckie recalls. "But he said that he really wanted to take me." Smiling, she adds: "I don't know why I said yes. There was just something in his voice."

Mike's risk paid off on that first date. "We just clicked," says Beckie. "I really liked what he had to say. There was an immediate attraction and respect because of the kind of work he was doing."

It didn't take long for Mike to realize he'd met the woman he wanted to spend the rest of his life with. But Beckie recalls that marriage wasn't an immediate goal for either one of them. "I was twenty-six and Michael was twenty-eight," she explains. "He was going to be this maverick lawyer and I kind of saw myself as someone who wanted to travel the world. That was how we planned on living our lives."

At the time, Beckie was committed to teaching in Japan for two years. From there, she planned to travel to China and Russia before settling down to teach in Norway. As for Mike, he was a confirmed bachelor—

complete with long working hours and a well-used Volkswagen that was barely big enough to hold a pair of skis. However, once Beckie had gone to Japan, he found that he deeply missed her. They kept in contact by letter and phone. When Beckie sent Mike a note to say that she had met someone else, he quickly formed a plan of action.

Later, he would write that he indulged in "about thirty seconds of self-pity" before enclosing a return ticket to Vancouver inside a ten-page letter explaining why they should stay together. It was typically Mike, both passionate and logical. "I think he ran it past all his lawyer buddies to make sure it made perfect sense," laughs Beckie. But it's the letter's heartfelt conviction she remembers most of all. "It was the kind of letter that was just impossible to resist," she confesses. They ended up meeting each other halfway in Hawaii, where they talked through their relationship. Shortly afterward, they decided to get married.

"Mike and I have the same values," says Beckie. "At the time, I didn't even realize just how much we had in common. He managed to articulate something that I hadn't really thought about. We share the kind of belief system that's worked for us from the very beginning. It has a lot to do with mutual respect, kindness, and listening to what the other person has to say."

∽⌒∾

An enduring love for the environment quickly proved to be one of the things that Beckie and Mike shared. In fact, the idea of getting a place where they could be closer to nature began to take shape while the couple honeymooned on the Sunshine Coast in 1971. Beckie was teaching school and Mike's political career had yet to take seed. Still "a gray flannel guerilla" on the fringes of power, the frenetic pace of public life was yet to come.

Asked about that period decades later, Mike and Beckie remember it as a time of endless possibilities. The couple honeymooned at Lord Jim's Lodge, just past Sechelt. "On our first night there Joni Mitchell was in the bar," recalls Beckie. "But it was like we were all there together and she was one of us." The Harcourts fondly remember Mitchell sending over a bottle of mead, thought to be good luck for newlyweds. It was all part of a very special time.

"Mike and I would walk these trails along the water, surrounded by arbutus trees." says Beckie. "It was just so beautiful. That's when I started looking."

During the early seventies, the couple was based in Vancouver and renting a small apartment in Kitsilano. Beckie worked as a teacher and Mike was rapidly gaining attention as a social activist who had been instrumental in stopping a freeway from cutting the city in half. His success in this matter marked the beginning of a new wave of thinking that would ultimately bring a fresh approach to Vancouver's future. But, at the time, Mike and Beckie weren't considering a life in politics.

"We were going to go back to the land," says Beckie. "He was going to be an Island lawyer in Victoria and I was going to be a part-time school-teacher. When Mike was elected to Vancouver city council as an alderman, they decided to stay in town. However, the idea of an island getaway still appealed to them. When Beckie noticed an ad in the paper listing lots for sale on Pender, they arranged to see them.

Both of them liked the properties they saw. But Beckie felt especially excited. "There were four or five people looking at the land and everyone started to talk about the parcel they wanted," she recalls. Suddenly, Beckie blurted out: "We'll take lot number four!"

Mike smiles, adding: "I remember turning around and saying: 'We'll what?'"

"We did talk about it, didn't we?" laughs Beckie. "Most of the time, we really do hear each other."

⌒⌒⌒

November 30 took on the eerie, warped timing of the truly terrifying. It was as if a number of small, isolated occurrences had somehow managed to come together in rapid succession, instantly conspiring to create the single darkest moment in Mike Harcourt's life.

It started with the slick deck. Mike's slippers began to slide out of control, unable to gain sufficient traction on the platform to regain proper footing. At the same time, the combined weight of the full buckets in either hand catapulted him forward in a motion as sudden as it was powerful and swift.

Mike recalls the terrible sensation of falling off the deck and down the rocky twenty-foot cliff as a brief instant. There was the feeling of tumbling down the punishing cliff. But he moved in and out of consciousness during the whole sequence of events. So much of what happened to him during the next few hours would never be totally clear in his mind. It was apparent that he had a concussion. That would prove the least worrisome legacy of the accident.

As a couple the Harcourts have worked hard at balancing various needs. Both of them have always felt the best way to reduce stress and anxiety throughout a hectic personal and political life is to share their feelings. Says Beckie: "We have a very transparent relationship."

Working at keeping the lines of communication open has always been a priority for both of them. During the first nine years of their marriage, as life became increasingly busy, they would create a yearly marriage contract. It was a concrete way of stopping to reflect on the priorities of their relationship as Beckie's teaching career flourished and Mike's political duties increased to the point where he worked ninety hours each week. The contract covered everything from major commitments to daily domestic chores.

Mike wanted his personal life to reflect the same sense of equality and openness he would bring to politics. "We started those contracts, partly as a result of my experiences as a family lawyer," he explains. "I discovered that what killed most relationships was the fact that people didn't communicate very well. They'd store stuff up and then explode with anger. The other party would be really hurt and they'd start firing these emotional bullets at each other. Things would get worse and worse until the relationship was destroyed, so we just decided to write it down.

"We spelled out what our goals were so that it was all clear," says Beckie. "It would take us months to work through—to get to the point where the other person was willing to sign. But, for a long time, it worked wonderfully well."

"Both of us are planners and list makers," adds Mike. "We've always believed in sorting out our priorities and directions by writing them down."

"We're very calm people by nature," observes Beckie. "We don't tend to flip out. And, when we do, it's a very rare thing. We like to think things through."

The contracts stopped shortly after their son Justen was born. "I think we just felt that we had it all down by that time," says Beckie. "We didn't need to spell out our marriage goals annually anymore."

At the same time, they never gave up on the idea of putting their thoughts down on paper. "Even when things would be really tough in our relationship, and we couldn't talk about it, we would write out what was bothering us," explains Beckie. "We would write out what was in our heart and on our mind and give that to the other person. It hasn't happened that many times in over thirty years of marriage, but it really helps to let the other person know exactly where you're at."

And yet, as Mike points out, they've always relied on different solutions to different problems. Both of them have learned that sometimes simply communicating isn't enough if they were going to ride out the stresses that politics put on marriage. "We've always been prepared to do big, bold things on the turn of a dime," he confides. "Sometimes, it's just like: 'Boom, okay let's do it.'"

Both of them point to 1976, which proved an especially trying year. Mike was involved in no less than three elections while they were in the process of renovating their Vancouver condo. "It was a mistake and we probably shouldn't have done it," says Mike of the renovation. "It was just a massive job. Plus it was very stressful in terms of getting into politics."

Near the end of the process, the strain on their relationship came to a head. Mike recalls arriving home one day to hear Beckie say, "Well, I can't take this anymore. I'm going travelling."

"I didn't even say that I couldn't take it anymore," remembers Beckie. "I just said: 'I'm leaving. I'm going to Europe.'"

Her husband's response? "I said: 'Oh, okay, let's sell the house and let's go.'" And that's exactly what they did. "That made everything fine," adds Beckie. "Mike listened to what I was saying and he instantly heard me."

⌒⌒⌒

The day-to-day world of politics provided its own unique stresses. As a couple, the Harcourts have developed the kind of emotional flexibility that's essential for a successful family life within the polarized and often volatile world of provincial politics in BC. Still, Beckie admits that there were times when the crueler demands of political life—having manure dumped on your front lawn or being subjected to nasty anonymous phone calls—would take their toll.

"I had a difficult time when Mike was premier," she says. "I used to put aside one day when I would fast, do my yoga, and meditate. That's kind of how I got through the political thing. I'd do those things and chill right out."

And yet, while Beckie found the life of a political spouse stressful, there was never any question that the results were worth the sacrifice. "I've been intimately involved with Mike's work for many years," she explains. "I've seen what goes into it and what he's trying to do. It means a lot to him and it's always meant a lot to me. I really believe in the value of what he does."

As for Mike, he'd characteristically managed to weather the stormier aspects of the premier's office by being what he termed "a cool guy in a hot province." Perhaps his greatest skill as a politician was the ability to create a consensus between the left and the right in order to achieve a positive result. To bring people together or, as he puts it, "connect all those disparate dots, take an idea and make it happen." As premier, one of his legacies was to double the amount of protected wilderness areas in BC. Along the way, one journalist described him as a man whose congeniality tends to mask his passion.

Mike was known for treating everyone with a basic friendliness and courtesy, regardless of their political stripe. He has written, "I'd rather not hurt anybody, not even in politics." Some members of the media considered his outlook a disadvantage in the often cutthroat world of backroom politics. But Mike managed to hang on to his ideals despite articles that characterized him as wishy-washy or too nice. "You have to be highly disciplined in politics," he observes. "It requires tremendous energy and endurance. If you don't have a strong constitution, it can be very hard on you."

Mike's political strength extended to his values as well. *Globe and Mail* editor Edward Greenspon would characterize him as "a thoroughly decent and almost serene man." What he didn't note was that the two qualities are intrinsically linked within Harcourt's personality. His calm demeanour stems directly from an unwavering sense of fairness and civility.

∽∾∾

There came a time when Mike Harcourt was convinced that the values he prized so highly had no place in "the blood sport" of BC politics. During his tenure as premier tension mounted over a scandal the media dubbed "Bingogate," the diversion of more than one million dollars in charity funds from the Nanaimo Commonwealth Holding Society into the pockets of others, most notably those of former NDP MLA Dave Stupich. The scandal took place long before Mike became premier and he would later be completely exonerated of any knowledge or connection to the situation by impartial investigators. But the continuing media pressure to bring someone down—a pressure that was mirrored by some NDP insiders—would not let up.

"I was disgusted with the feeding frenzy of the media as well as with the behaviour of certain members of the NDP and the trade union movement," he says. "They didn't want a trial or whatever. They just wanted somebody to suffer some consequences, to be hung from the hanging tree. I just kept getting angrier and angrier. Things were building up to quite a pitch."

For a politician who always tried to keep a cool head, the anger and disgust was a warning sign. Mike would pay attention to what his emotions were telling him, but his biggest concern was the effect the ongoing media blitz was having on Beckie and Justen as well as his elderly parents. He also knew that if he stayed in office it could have a negative effect on his party.

"I'm not the sort of person who tortures himself with indecision," he explains. "I like to take in the information, weigh my options, and make the best possible choice." For Mike, the choice seemed clear—both for himself and for his family. The man who once observed that "politics is all about sacrifice" would resign.

Later, Mike would say: "I took a bullet for the New

Democratic Party and, in a sense, for British Columbia." But it was also true that once the choice was made, the wound began to heal almost immediately. "It took a couple of months for the disgust to dissipate," he says. "After that, I could watch the way things unfolded without feeling stressed about it."

Shortly after his resignation in 1995, Mike would begin work on his book, *A Measure of Defiance*. It was his chance to set his political legacy as mayor and premier on the record. It was also an uncompromising look at media ethics. Many were surprised by the work's tough stance on such issues as "pack journalism." But, for Mike, the book was largely therapeutic. "Writing allowed me to get all my feelings out on paper," he confesses. "Once you do that, it's very cathartic. All the negative things were gone."

Mike's decision to resign bore fruit in other ways as well. He was offered a position at the University of British Columbia where he could concentrate on issues of sustainable development. Prime Minister Chrétien appointed him to the National Round Table on the Environment and the Economy. He worked on building quality housing on Vancouver's Eastside. It was a happy and fulfilling time. "I've found a way of doing what needs to be done without all the hassle," he would observe.

On TV talk shows, he would jokingly refer to himself as "a recovering politician." Away from the political banquet circuit, he was able to improve his diet, work out regularly at the gym, and go jogging every other day with Beckie. "I was," he says, "in the best shape of my life." Most importantly, he could spend more time with his family. One of the perks of leaving full-time politics was that it allowed Mike and Beckie to spend more time at their place on Pender.

ȣ

One thing Mike understood immediately after tumbling off the deck. He was gravely injured.

"I remember lying stunned at the bottom of the cliff—face down in the water," he says. "I knew I couldn't move very well." He was in extreme shock, the threat of drowning so real that he could almost feel it in his presence. And then another thought registered and he hung onto it as if it were a lifeline.

"I thought, 'This is such a pedestrian way to die.' I mean, who expected it? I just went to fill up the hot tub and suddenly this is *it*."

The thought forced him into action. "I basically said to myself, 'Hell, no. I'm not going to go this way, so I hauled back and tried to yell for Beckie. I don't know how I did it. But that's probably the impulse that saved my life because I was able to lift my head long enough to get some breath."

However, in terms of summoning Beckie, the gesture proved futile. She was at the far end of the cottage and the waves were crashing so loudly they drowned out Mike's cries for help. There was no way she could hear him and Mike knew that he could only keep his head above water for so long. "If it wasn't for what happened next," he recalls, "I would have died."

Both Mike and Beckie consider what then happened a miracle. Beckie chose that moment to go looking for Mike. What she initially saw—Mike's empty slipper and one bucket—alerted her to the danger. After that, she looked over the edge of the deck and saw Mike lying face down in the water. "I thought he was dead," she says. "That was my first thought."

Then, she didn't think at all. "It was like my body and mind instantly jumped into gear," she remembers.

There was no clear path down to the beach from the Harcourts' cottage, so Beckie had to take the long way around, to reach a neighbour's path two hundred yards from their place. It seemed an eternity. "I just kept running," she recalls. "Running and praying."

When Beckie got down to the beach, Mike was lying with his face fully submerged in water. She waded into the sea and tried immediately to turn her unconscious husband over. She's a petite woman and—even with adrenaline pumping through her—it proved far from easy. "I was using all my strength," she says. "And the tide was coming in."

She finally managed to turn Mike over. His head was bruised, his face, blue and bloody. But Beckie concentrated on clearing the water and debris from his mouth with her fingers. "He made a sound," she says. "I remember him making a sound."

She knew she had to prop him up somehow because the tide was rising. She tried to use different kinds of sticks that she was pulling from the water, but they were too small. Finally she found a piece of driftwood in the water that was the right size and placed it under Mike's head like a pillow. "I don't know how I did that," she remarks. "I don't know how I managed to get Michael in the right position." But Beckie did know two things. Her husband was alive and she had to get help.

2

THE JOURNEY BEGINS

---

*"Lots of times you're getting called out at all hours
of the night and it can be pretty tough on family
life. But when you're out there, doing your best and
able to help somebody, that's the reward."*
— STEVE WINDSOR, NORTH PENDER FIRE CHIEF IN 2002

North Pender fire chief Steve Windsor took Beckie's
call. A veteran rescue worker who'd been involved in
several fire departments over the years, he'd lived on
the island long enough to know almost everybody.
There was usually a personal connection between a
caller and one of the department's members, especially when things slowed down in the off-season. That
was part of what made a tightly knit community like
Pender special. Islanders depended much more on each
other, but they cared more for each other too.

Windsor always felt that the most rewarding part of
his job on Pender was being able to assist his neighbours when they needed him the most. "Lots of times

you're getting called out at all hours of the night and it can be pretty tough on family life," he says of rescue work. "But when you're out there, doing your best and able to help somebody, that's the reward."

Windsor explains that you can never be certain what the outcome of any call will be. However, on this particular day, he would pick up the phone at around 1:00 P.M. and cast a lifeline that the Harcourts will remember for the rest of their lives.

✿

As soon as Beckie determined that Mike's head was able to remain positioned above the water line, she ran back up to the cottage to call for help. "It seemed to take forever," she says, although she was climbing and running as fast as she could. There was no time to consider either the importance or the sheer physical challenge of what she had just done. Within minutes, her body had gone into overdrive—running hundreds of yards from their cottage and then scrambling around a steep, slippery series of rocks that offered dangerously precarious footing. From there, she had braved the thigh-deep water to get next to Mike at the base of the cliff. The most crucial piece of information had registered quickly. He couldn't move his legs.

Later, there would be time to ponder what she had managed to accomplish against all odds. At one hundred and twenty pounds, she had somehow succeeded in turning her two-hundred-and-fifteen-pound husband over and get him breathing. It took several tries to make this happen. Mike's sweatshirt and jeans were waterlogged and Beckie's footing in the water was precarious. At the same time, she was desperately trying to get a response from him. He'd suffered a concussion and his face had turned blue from exposure to the frigid water and bloody from multiple cuts and abrasions. As members of the rescue team would later say, many people in Beckie's position would have frozen in panic.

However, Beckie hung on to one thought. "I was screaming at Michael," she says. "The whole time I was calling his name. And the fact that, from somewhere in there, he heard me enough to make this sound—I knew he was alive. I thought that was a miracle."

There's no question that Beckie's timely arrival, combined with her quick response to the situation, lay at the very heart of that miracle. Veteran rescue workers from the North Pender Volunteer Fire Department would openly express their admiration for the daunting nature of her achievement. Doctors would subsequently tell Beckie that if she'd hesitated in her immediate response to get to her husband—frozen, fainted, or paused to make the emergency call before running down to the water—he would have died. Later, when Mike was able to fully comprehend everything that had happened, he would refer to Beckie as his guardian angel.

To this day, Beckie is uncertain why she made the right choice. Maybe it was simply the loving urge to instantly move forward—to get next to her injured husband so they could face what had happened together. Whatever the reason, Beckie met the crisis head on. "When I was running along the cliff to get to the little path that runs off the beach, I was wondering whether I should have gone in and called 911 first," she recalls. "I don't know whether it was just instinct. I was just grateful to be able to run."

Making the decision to run toward her husband and save his life was only part of the battle. Afterwards, wet, cold, and shaken, Beckie had to retrace the difficult path in reverse in order to make the emergency call from the cottage. She struggled to remain as calm and lucid as possible as she dialled 911.

Beckie would return to Mike with towels and blankets, doing her best to keep him comfortable. Mike would subsequently say that he remembered Beckie calling his name repeatedly and trying to keep him warm. It was the brightest piece in a frightening puzzle of memory that would return in jagged pieces. Along with the feeling of plunging into the frigid water and being unable to move his legs, hands, and fingers.

⚮

Steve Windsor remembers that Beckie sounded distraught yet focused. After supplying the necessary information, she also had the presence of mind to call her neighbour, Allen Rollie, who would direct members of the fire department rescue team to the scene. As luck would have it, there was a training course at the fire station and all the personnel were gathered in the same place. Thanks to this—and the fact that the fire department had been trained in the appropriate emergency medical procedures—the rescue process would begin mere minutes after Beckie's alert.

Falls are not an uncommon occurrence for a rescue team to respond to, even in a small community like Pender. Windsor was one of the first rescue personnel on the scene, and when he started to take in the details of this particular accident, his initial feeling was a sense of amazement at Mike's survival. The fall off the cliff could have easily proved fatal. But, thanks to Beckie's quick actions, Mike had managed to avoid the next potential fatality as well: drowning. As Windsor would tell a reporter: "He's very, very lucky. I'd say he probably hit that one in one hundred chance of surviving."

While Mike's face had taken a bloody beating from the rocks and his head had initially been submerged in water, Beckie's rescue meant that he was able to begin breathing regularly again. Investigators would later speculate on another piece of good fortune within the arc of the accident. Judging from some broken branches, it's almost certain that Mike briefly collided with a cedar tree near the edge of the cliff, which helped to slow down the momentum of his fall.

But, despite being lucky enough to survive, Mike's immediate situation presented a definite challenge from a rescue standpoint. Pender's isolated beauty— the very thing that had attracted the Harcourts to the spot in the first place—would now pose a hindrance to the rescue effort. The rescue team had to deal with a shale cliff that led straight down to the rocks. From a distance, the cliff can look majestic. However, as one member of the team remarked, the cliff situation was pretty ugly from a rescuer's perspective.

As Windsor explains, the initial concern was not only how Mike had fallen but where. "Normally, you don't have to deal with getting into a place that's so inaccessible," he says. "It just adds another dimension to the whole thing."

Inaccessibility wasn't the only problem. Nobody had actually witnessed Mike's accident—and it's estimated that Beckie came to her husband's rescue within a crucial window of only a few minutes after the fall—piecing together what actually happened left little room for optimism.

❧

Mike would later describe his horrific fall as "my collision with the rocks." Although the phrase partially summarizes the terrible punishment his body endured, it doesn't begin to capture the bizarre nature of the fall itself, a tumble whose terrible momentum would take him off the deck, past the back lawn, and over the cliff before he finally landed on the rocks.

"I remember slipping and stumbling," he would say. "But I had no idea how I could have gone five feet off the deck and the fifteen feet to the cliff edge and over the cliff."

All the emergency observers could do at first was estimate the severity of the fall. Windsor's guess was that Mike's tumble covered the fifteen feet to the edge of the cliff before he dropped to the rocky shoreline below on the awful momentum of a hard bounce. For the time being, the damage to his body would prove impossible to fully calculate.

No one had time to contemplate the terrible irony of the situation. Part of the reason Mike had left full-time politics was to give his personal life its due after so many years of public service. He wanted to spend more time with his family and more time playing the sports he loved. He made the change because, as he has written, "when we are honest with ourselves, we must admit that our lives are all that really belong to us." Only minutes before, he had been focused on the familiar rituals of his favourite place and actively enjoying one of the happiest periods in his life. Now, propped up at the bottom of a cliff, there was a real question as to how much of that life he actually had left.

❧❧❧

Windsor knew that he had to get immediate medical aid down to Mike in order to staunch the bleeding from the cuts on his head and legs and treat the effects of hypothermia that resulted from his plunge into the cold water. He also realized that he needed to get a spine board down to Mike to stabilize his injury. "When you take a fall from that height, you automatically assume that there's a neck or back injury," says Windsor. "In this case we knew that Mike couldn't move his legs. So we had to get people and equipment down there as quickly as possible. It's much easier than trying to bring him out."

One member of the rescue team took the path that Beckie had used to gain access to Mike. Seeing how cumbersome and time-consuming this was, two other team members, who specialized in steep descents, used climbing ropes to rappel down the face of the cliff. As Windsor explains, this was just one of many decisions designed to facilitate the speed of Mike's rescue.

"If you have people standing around and scratching their heads, that's a waste," he remarks. "That's why the training is such a critical component in any volunteer fire department. You really have to have people who can step right in and do the series of things that are required for a specific predicament."

Mike received attention from the team in short order. But when Windsor and the others discovered the shape he was in—immobile and in a state of shock that rendered him incoherent—they felt a mutual sense of foreboding.

Things were complicated by the fact that the accident scene was becoming increasingly crowded. Beckie thought it best to get out of the way and let the rescue team do its job, so she made the difficult decision to watch from the cliff. Much later, members of the rescue squad would share their private thoughts with her. "They didn't think he'd make it off the cliff," she says. "They just didn't think he'd make it."

By the time the fire department rescue squad had completed its initial evaluation of Mike's condition, the Pender unit of the BC Ambulance Service had arrived at the accident site. Immersed in calf-deep water, they put a neck brace on Mike and immobilized him by placing him on a spine board. From this point on, it would be vital to keep Mike's movement to a minimum.

Given the nature of Mike's condition, Windsor was reluctant to risk further injury by pulling him up the cliff on a stretcher. "The goal is to get the person out without doing any further damage," he explains. "Rope rescue bumps a person around because there's more movement involved." Looking for the best alternative, Windsor decided it would be wise to try to get Mike out by boat.

"With Pender, there are a number of properties that are bordering on water," says Windsor. "The coast guard, the coast guard auxiliary, and even the RCMP are equipped with boats. And, as a fire department, we're trained in the boat rescue angle as well. In the past, we've managed to get people out of some difficult situations using this method."

Windsor put a call out to both the coast guard and its auxiliary. Then the fire department crew immediately started to rig up the ropes, just in case it became necessary to pull Mike up the cliff in a basket stretcher.

"That's part of our training," explains Windsor. "You plan for contingencies. If they get back to us ten minutes later and say that they can't get a boat to us, you better have a backup plan. You can't sit there for half an hour, twiddling your thumbs and waiting for the next boat."

Fortunately, there was a coast guard vessel from Salt Spring Island in the area. The Ganges Coast Guard cutter the *Skua* arrived on the scene at 2:20 P.M., anchoring offshore. Two crew members arrived on the accident site using a high-speed inflatable boat commonly known as a Zodiac. The two ambulance attendants would join Mike and the members of the coast guard crew in the boat. A member of the fire department rescue squad drove the ambulance the short distance to the rendezvous point of the Hope Bay dock. By this time, Mike was verbalizing more coherently than a few minutes beforehand. He repeatedly asked where he was and would retain a clear memory of the coast guard crew lifting him into the boat.

"The coast guard guys didn't know who I was," Mike would later recall. "They were just doing their usual extraordinary job. And then they got me on the Zodiac and put me on the dock. One of them turned to the other and said: 'Is that who I think it is?'"

Mike's head was scarred and he would later describe his condition as "bloodied and battered." Members of the coast guard would express doubt about his ability to make it to the hospital alive. If he was lucky enough to survive the next few hours, they didn't hold up much hope of Mike surviving the next few days. But thanks to the speed of the operation, they had little time to ponder such dark thoughts.

Once again there was no room for Beckie on the emergency transport. But there was no time to waste. Beckie would make a quick change out of her wet clothes and drive the family Volvo to the Pender Island medical clinic in the company of neighbour Allen Rollie.

From the Hope Bay dock, Mike would proceed to the Pender Island medical clinic by ambulance. It was a relatively short journey, just a few minutes from start to finish. But as the ambulance sped toward the clinic another kind of journey began. Mike had always had a strong ethical commitment to the principles of a first-rate medical system; he would now experience that system from a different perspective, a first-hand one rather than an abstract one. Mike's accident would begin an intimate relationship with a series of medical and health professionals who would strive to help him through the greatest crisis of his life.

∽⌒∾

On a typical day, weekenders would come in to be treated by Dr. Don Williams for a bee sting, a cut, or a broken arm. Affectionately known as "Dr. Don," his nickname has always served to make patients feel a little more at ease. "Everybody calls me Dr. Don," he says, explaining that his last name can be hard for kids to say. "It's always felt right to me. I think it makes it easier for some people if they can establish a less formal connection that way."

This was the first physician Mike would see in the wake of his fall—a semi-retired general practitioner who has been treating patients on the island since 1987. Over the years, the two men had gotten to know each other through their mutual bond with the island. "We're both reasonably long-term Pender Islanders," says Williams. "We've done some fundraising for a community hall and a piece of marshland called Medicine Beach, which was going to be developed but is now a park."

Asked his opinion of Mike, Dr. Williams observes that he's never been the kind of man who lets his ego get in the way of relating to people. "With a lot of politicians the phrase 'messiah complex' comes to mind," he remarks. "But with Mike there's a genuine humility. Despite his large size, there's this gentleness." In turn, Mike would later refer to Williams as "not only a terrific doctor but a friend."

It says a lot about Williams that he downplays his personal role in both the emergency preparations he would set in motion and the crucial medical treatment he would administer upon Mike's arrival. "Any of the doctors I work with on Pender would have done a very good job in the same situation," Williams modestly opines. "But I hope it was some comfort to Mike that I wasn't a stranger."

It's the statement of a man who clearly values the human element in his medical practice. "I quite love what I do," he says. "This is a small enough community that you get to know a lot of people on a personal level. And, for some, it's nice to have an acquaintance with their doctor—some sort of recognition that you're going to do your best for them.

"I've always worked in small towns," he adds. "I consider it a special privilege. I think you can do more for people if you know a little bit about their family, their background, and where they work. It's a myth that doctors don't make house calls anymore. I visit the homes of my patients frequently."

For Williams, the relationship he develops with his patients is an important aspect of practising rural medicine. Part of British Columbia's rural locum program—where he fills in for physicians who are on holiday or taking a course—he also enjoys the challenge of treating a wide spectrum of medical concerns. This includes emergency treatment, often without the luxury of being in ready communication with a large urban hospital. "You just can't call a specialist up," says Williams. "So you have to be able to do everything from treating heart attacks and strokes to spinal cord injuries."

❦

Dr. Williams—who happened to be on call the Saturday afternoon Mike fell off his deck—was informed of the accident via his pager. He received a short message that provided few details. Their long acquaintance aside, Williams would have no difficulty treating Mike's case with the necessary impartiality an emergency of this nature requires. "When you're deal-

ing with trauma and it's someone you know you immediately go into a certain mode," he remarks. "You can't
allow the relationship to intrude and become an emotional factor. It's just part of your training."

As Williams explains, a spinal cord injury is anything but a common occurrence on a place like Pender.
"It's quite rare," he observes. "I would say a rural doctor might see one case every five to ten years. It might
happen a little more often in a skiing area where people take falls. But in my seventeen years of practice
here, that's just about the right average."

And yet, like all physicians who work in emergency
departments, Dr. Williams regularly keeps himself ap-
prised of the latest developments in trauma medicine
through various courses and updates. His knowledge of
the current theories regarding spinal cord injuries as
well as his ability to quickly access where Mike would
need to go for the next crucial phase of his treatment
would ultimately prove invaluable.

Prior to Mike's accident, Williams notes that the
last two neck injuries he can recall happening on
Pender were both fatal. "This is a very serious type of
injury," he explains. Despite the brevity of the message
he received about Mike on his pager, the doctor determined that it would be best to transfer him as quickly
as possible to the Vancouver General Hospital. So the
first thing he did, after getting the message, was to call
the hospital's spinal cord unit. Dr. Williams consulted
with other physicians, including Dr. Marcel Dvorak,
who Mike would later refer to as "probably the best

spinal cord surgeon in the country." Dvorak—well known locally as the specialist who operated on Vancouver Canuck forward Daniel Sedin after he was injured at the 2000 World Hockey Championships—happened to be on call that weekend at VGH. It was decided that Mike should travel to Vancouver via emergency helicopter as soon as Dr. Williams could examine him.

∽⌒∾

What is always important about these types of injuries is the time element, explains Williams. "We're trying to get the patient to the right doctor—make phone calls to the specialist and transport them quickly. They need to get the right scans and the right surgical procedures rapidly."

Dr. Williams wanted to take advantage of the fact that—thanks to the skill of the rescuers and more than a little luck—the time element seemed to be working in Mike's favour. "The first responders here—the ambulance crew and the emergency staff—are top notch," he says. "And the coast guard got over here in a real hurry. When you combine that with Beckie's quick action, you have a series of very lucky events following on the heels of the accident."

The relatively smooth succession of events hit a snag when Dr. Williams discovered that there wasn't an available bed in the spinal unit. "There was some resistance because the spinal cord unit was full," he recalls. "I had to do a little leaning and it took a little work. But, when all is said and done, it doesn't matter who it was. If they were going to go there, they were going to get a bed."

In such situations, time can be your enemy. Dr. Williams would have approximately fifteen minutes to examine Mike—to make sure that there were no unforeseen injuries that could possibly delay his departure. After that, the helicopter would be hovering over the local elementary school, which Windsor and other members of the team had transformed into a makeshift landing area.

Fortunately, Dr. Williams' persistence would pay off. With the help of physicians readying things on the mainland, a bed in the spinal cord unit was prepared for Mike's arrival. Shortly after that Mike was wheeled into the clinic by the ambulance attendants. Even before Dr. Williams could see Mike, he could hear the familiar sound of his voice.

"No matter what level of injury you're getting, the first and most important thing is to make sure the patient is breathing properly," he says. "So the fact that I could hear Mike's voice was a pretty good sign. It was clear to me that his respiration was adequate."

After monitoring his breathing and assessing the condition of Mike's lungs, the doctor found he could communicate with his patient quite easily. Among other things, this meant that Mike's concussion didn't appear to be highly significant at that point. "He was mildly hypothermic and also mildly confused," Williams recalls. "But he was putting sentences together and seemed fairly coherent."

After his initial examination, Williams made the decision to administer a powerful steroidal drug called methylprednisolone. Since the 1990s, studies have indicated that—if the drug can be administered within hours of the accident—it may reduce damage to the cells as well as improve the patient's ability to move and perceive sensation.

"At this point, administering the drug is standard procedure for spinal cord injuries," says Williams, who kept the drug in stock for just such an emergency. "The theory behind administering this powerful steroid is that it very rapidly reduces the swelling around the injured spinal cord, which is being deprived of blood flow, so you don't get the same amount of damage."

The goal in giving Mike the drug was to extend what Williams refers to as his "window of opportunity"—the time frame in which the patient can be treated. Williams offers that Mike's window may very well have been extended in two ways—getting the drug and the fact that he was suffering from hypothermia. As the doctor explains, Mike's exposure to the cold water could have been a blessing in disguise.

"Mike had been outside and in the water long enough for his body temperature to be reduced," he observes. "And that can prolong the life of the cells, particularly in the central nervous system. So his low body temperature was actually serendipitous. I think it may have very well been one of the factors that was in play for him."

◡᷐᷒᷒◠

Mike's positive attitude in the face of so much shock and uncertainty was another factor that Dr. Williams felt would inevitably make a significant difference. As the doctor notes, Mike's response differed from that of the average patient in a similar situation.

"He was completely co-operative, absolutely helpful, and not demanding of anything," says Williams. "But to me, what's quite astounding is that he came in with a sense of relative optimism right from the start. He just wasn't going to let it get him down, which is remarkable considering the fact that he had a really significant trauma."

Dr. Williams, who notes that he has a strong interest in behavioural science, says that he feels a patient's attitude plays a vital role in dealing with illness. "If I know anything in thirty-five years of practice, it's that people with a positive approach do better," he explains. "It doesn't matter how you measure it. Their immunity is stronger, they heal faster, and they do better psychologically. Unfortunately, the converse is also true."

"The power of the psyche is absolutely phenomenal," he adds. "It works in such strange and mysterious ways. But, if you can help people access that, it's such a profound and powerful tool. Part of the art of medicine—and one of the lovely things about it—is to spot that power in a person and to help them open that door, to help them recognize it and use it to their advantage."

On that Saturday afternoon, as the helicopter was landing to take Mike on the next phase of his journey, Dr. Williams had no doubt that his patient's emotional stamina would prove his most valuable attribute on the difficult road ahead. "Mike's a really spirited person," he says. "It's just the way he lives his life. The eternal optimism, the ability to rise to the challenge whether it's personal or larger. The difference that these qualities can make are not only huge but humbling."

∽∽∽

Like Mike, Beckie tried to dwell on hopeful thoughts. When she rendezvoused with Mike at the Pender Island clinic, she recalls, she felt relieved to know that he was in the right place. She also found being able to discuss the right course of action with Dr. Williams comforting. But none of what followed would have been possible if she had not decided to look for Mike instead of returning to the garden. Over the next few weeks, she would reflect on why she had chosen that particular time to go searching for Mike. It was, after all, a seemingly ordinary day in a place where time unfolds at a much slower pace. Why had she acted at that moment? Was Beckie's impulse a question of fate, instinct, or—as their friend, lawyer, and author Tom Berger, would later write in a letter—an example that "coincidence is God's way of remaining anonymous."

Could it be that Beckie knew Mike so well that, on a subconscious level she could sense her husband was in danger? The cottage's generous windows allow an expansive view of the outdoors. Beckie was shuttling back and forth between their home and the garden. In the back of her mind, she may have been aware that she hadn't seen Mike in a while. Whatever the reason, Beckie would be forever grateful for the impulse that saved her husband's life. Instead of returning to the garden, she turned and went around the house to look for Mike. "I don't know what it was," she would say, when asked to speculate on the urge to seek out Mike. "There was just this feeling that I had to find him."

Later, she would be thankful for the way her body and mind had responded. "I've always felt that you need to have a clear mind and a healthy body," she confides. "You need to look after yourself because you never know when you're really going to have to reach deep.

"Most of the time, we can sort of operate in neutral and cope with what we need to do in life on a daily basis," she adds. "It's not like we have to have this really intense focus all the time. But you've got to look after yourself because you just never know when you're going to be faced with something like this."

⌀⌀⌀⌀

For Beckie one of the most difficult parts of that day was Mike's flight to Vancouver. Because there wasn't enough room in the helicopter, she had to take the long, lonely trip to the mainland by ferry with her car. There are only a couple of ferry crossings to Vancouver on a fall Saturday. That fateful November 30, the next ferry from Pender was the last one of the day, and the two-and-a-half-hour journey unfortunately included a stop at Galiano Island. To make matters worse, the handful of Pender passengers were informed of a delay due to the fog that had descended around Galiano.

"We couldn't leave for a while," Beckie says. "So I just had to find a way to keep myself together. If my thoughts wandered, I'd just get really scared. I'd start to shake." Beckie decided to clear her mind and focus on her breathing. Doing this, helped her to remain relatively calm. When she had to focus on a thought, it was always the same one: *My husband is alive and I am grateful.* As the helicopter made its way to VGH, Mike did his best to focus on the same thing.

3

SCRAP PLAN A

"Go for it. And I hope to see you in the morning."
— MIKE HARCOURT TO SPINAL SURGEON MARCEL DVORAK

For Beckie, the ferry trip presented the first of many challenges she would face during the coming months. The farther away the boat sailed from Pender, the farther away Beckie was moving from the gardening gloves and freshly harvested vegetables she had abandoned outside the cottage. Like the overturned bucket that lay near Mike's forgotten slipper, they were tangible symbols of a happy and productive life that had suddenly spilled over into the unknown.

Beckie struggled to keep fear at bay. She got out of her car during the ferry journey and found a quiet spot where she could focus on her breathing. "There were so many things for me to be worried about," she says of that period. "There were times when I would catch myself getting very scared. But I just decided that I would try my best not to do that. Whenever I caught myself going to that scary place, I'd think, I can't be here. If I do this to myself, I'm going to have a breakdown."

The only thing she felt certain was that they would have to learn to endure constant change. "We had no expectations about what we would get back from our previous life," she explains. "I think we both instantly understood that our previous life was done. That we were going to have to pour all our energy into each day just to stay on track with our new life."

One overwhelming fact about her husband would also provide some consolation. "Mike has this core of steel," she says. "He's very tough when he needs to be. It's something he gets from his dad."

꧁꧂

Mike has always been very proud of his parents, Frank and Stella Harcourt, for both their kindness and generosity to others and also for their enduring determination to get the most from each new day. Frank recently passed away at the age of ninety-one, but Mike's mother is still thriving. After the accident Stella would regularly take a taxi to the hospital to visit Mike. He confides that she and his father "were always very tough-minded as well as bringing this kind of fierce energy to life. I guess there's a bit of that in me too."

One of the greatest lessons Mike learned from his dad was the way Frank built on the hard lessons of his childhood to make a better life for himself. "My dad's father left the family when my dad was a year old," Mike explains. "His mother raised five kids all by herself. She held down two jobs. She had her own millinery shop in the Hotel Vancouver and she was the head matron at Oakalla prison. She died when dad was seventeen, so he was basically left on his own with four brothers and sisters."

Frank married Stella at the height of the Depression. Together, they traveled across the Prairies while Frank sold magazine subscriptions and lessons in diesel mechanics to farmers in the middle of plowing their fields. Success at describing the wonders of *Maclean's* meant the difference between sleeping in the car on an empty stomach and being able to afford the luxury of dinner and a hotel bed. According to Mike, this job really honed his dad's people skills. "He'd load up the car and head out," explains Mike. "He had absolutely no money, but there was no way he was going to let that stop him."

And yet, despite Frank's difficult life, he never became judgmental or bitter. "After surviving the Depression, he survived being a lieutenant on a destroyer escort, looking for Nazi submarines in the North Atlantic," says Mike. "After that, he survived thirty years of corporate wars selling insurance. But as a dad, he was never domineering in terms of giving out orders. He cared but he had a very unobtrusive kind of presence."

Mike paints a picture of a loving father who taught his son to cherish life on a number of levels, giving him a sense of place and teaching him to value humanity. "He always cared for people and he always cared for Vancouver," Mike explains. "He was never working just to make a buck. He always said, 'I don't sell insurance. I look after people's needs.' And people trusted him implicitly. He literally helped thousands of people and, to this day, many of them still come up and tell me so."

Mike confides that he also learned many valuable life lessons from his mother, not the least of which was learning to care for others. "My mother is a very strong Christian," he says. "The United Church has always been a big part of her life. I picked up a strong sense of social justice from her."

Frank and Stella also gently guided Mike as he figured out his own needs. From an early age, he would be raised to make his own choices. "Basically, my parents gave me a huge amount of freedom just to be and do whatever I wanted," Mike recalls. His upbringing would prepare him for making tough decisions throughout his life as well as teaching him to count his blessings.

While he lay motionless in a hospital bed on the evening of November 30, Mike was drawing on the strength of that upbringing.

∞

As a distraught Beckie made her way from the ferry to the hospital, she understood that it was important to remain focused. At this time there were many more questions about Mike's condition than answers. And she needed to have a clear mind, unhampered by distracting thoughts.

"I knew that I had to try and stay in the present from the very beginning of the accident," she explains. "I just felt like all my focus needed to be on the here and now. There would be so much happening and so much information to take in that I couldn't afford not to be with it. I needed to hear what people were saying."

Like Mike, Beckie has always considered accurate information the tool needed in order to make the right decision. Even in her agitated state, Beckie realized she would require help to fully interpret and comprehend Mike's medical diagnosis. She didn't want to risk missing anything important at this crucial stage.

With this in mind, she had made a call on her cellphone to her longtime Vancouver friend Barb Cochrane. Barb is the wife of Dr. Doug Cochrane, a pediatric neurosurgeon and the former chief surgeon at BC's Children's Hospital. Mrs. Cochrane, who was on her way back from Kelowna, where she was supervising the construction of the family's summer home, immediately called her husband, who then met Beckie at VGH.

The Harcourts have known the Cochranes since 1986 when they first became neighbours. At the time, Beckie was teaching school and Mike was gearing up for provincial politics. "They were right next door," recalls Beckie. "I remember seeing Barb moving the furniture all by herself because Doug was at the hospital. I thought, I can relate to somebody like that, so we became friends."

The friendship grew over the years, helped along by the fact that the Cochranes had a daughter close to Justen's age. In fact, Doug and Barb would ultimately become Justen's godparents. "They adored Justen," explains Beckie. "They were thrilled to become his godparents. It just made us feel really good." Those warm feelings were returned by the Cochranes, so it wasn't surprising that Doug found the news of Mike's accident unsettling.

On the way to the hospital, Dr. Cochrane had only a sketchy knowledge of Mike's situation. The only thing he really knew was that his friend of many years had been seriously injured in a fall. "It was certainly a time of anxiety," says Doug, who would arrive at the hospital within twenty minutes of his wife's call. "I felt that on the one hand I knew too little and, on the other hand, I knew too much."

However, when he was admitted to VGH, a few elements were definitely on Mike's side. Like Dr. Williams, Dr. Cochrane felt that the rescue team's excellent work was clearly in Mike's favour. "We have a very good first responder system in BC," he says. "In some respects, the outcome of Mike's kind of injury is determined by the effectiveness of the ambulance system and the paramedics. I believe they made a great difference."

Dr. Cochrane also points out that Mike would benefit from certain high-tech refinements that were unavailable only a few years before his accident. Through the latest advances in computerized (axial) tomography and magnetic resonance imaging—often respectively referred to as a CT scan and an MRI—doctors would be able to attain the sort of detailed images that would greatly aid in pinpointing the nature of Mike's injury. "These investigative tools are really quite significant when it comes to the prognostication of a spinal patient's recovery," Dr. Cochrane emphasizes.

But such tools are only as good as the highly skilled people who employ them.

⌒⌒⌒

Both Mike and Beckie readily agree that one of their best pieces of luck was that Dr. Marcel Dvorak was on call that weekend. A rugged, handsome man in his mid-forties, Dr. Dvorak is considered one of the world's top spinal surgeons. The proud father of six kids, he's also quick to point out the accomplishments of his professional family, a team of spine surgeons that service the spinal care needs of the three to four million people who live in British Columbia.

"We have a dedicated group of six spine surgeons here," he says. "Some are neurosurgeons, some are orthopedic surgeons, but we're all equally excited, motivated, and driven. We work together and we all get along together, which is unique."

Originally, Dr. Dvorak wanted to train in another surgical specialty. It was Dr. Clive Duncan—his professor and currently a professor of Orthopedics at the

University of British Columbia—who encouraged Marcel to consider specializing in spinal surgery.

"My immediate reaction was not a chance," he recalls. "I felt it was way too high-risk. But then we talked and I really thought about it. I agreed to do it and, since then, I clearly feel I've made the right decision."

"I've got a passion for what I do," he says. "I just love it." He laughs adding, "I probably love it too much. That's one of my wife's comments. She thinks I get a little too much gratification out of my work."

For Dr. Dvorak, the appeal of spinal surgery is that it brings together a number of elements that he finds gratifying. "It's a combination of things," he says. "The technical fascination with the procedure, the instrumentation and the surgery itself, combined with the ability to share so profoundly in someone's life. It's great. Where else do you get to be involved with people at such a profound moment of crisis in their lives?" he asks. "To develop the level of trust where people allow you to do something to them while they're asleep. To operate and to be able to make their spine straighter or make them pain-free. There's nothing else like it."

∽∾∾

Doug arrived at VGH around 6 P.M., followed shortly thereafter by Barb. Beckie would arrive two hours later, straight from the ferry. Barb and Doug would wait for a total of three and a half hours before being allowed to see Mike. "We were sitting around waiting for him to arrive," Doug recalls. "And, more importantly, sitting around waiting for someone to talk to us afterwards. It was very wearing." All this while Mike was getting settled into his new surroundings, and the required tests were being done to get an accurate diagnosis of his injury.

During the wait, a number of things ran through Dr. Cochrane's mind. As a close friend, he couldn't help but wonder how drastically the accident would change the Harcourts' lives. As a physician, he knew all too well what the consequences could be.

"I thought, How are we going to reconstruct their home? Where would they move to?" he confides. "I was envisioning life from a wheelchair. And, having treated many patients like Mike, I know what that means to the lives of the patient and everyone around them. I think, for anybody, it would be so life-altering as to be incomprehensible."

There were many reasons to be worried. Only a few hours earlier, Mike had been a healthy, active man, who was happily contemplating nothing more challenging than an invigorating afternoon of work in the garden. Now, several problems were combining to lower his resistance and make him disturbingly frail, all of them serious and of immediate concern.

Things looked grim. But, for the Harcourts, the constant support of Doug and Barb Cochrane would prove invaluable. "Doug just became so 'hands on' with us," says Beckie. "He guided us in so many areas, almost without us noticing that we were being guided."

For Doug, it was an easy choice to make. Asked his opinion of Mike Harcourt as a person, he stresses his friend's ongoing concern for those struggling to cope with life. "Mike has always derived great joy in helping those who are less fortunate," he observes. "If you look at what's driven many aspects of his life from the time he was a storefront lawyer, it's the idea that more can be done for the benefit of others—more can be given. He's always built things based on that feeling." Now Mike was the one who needed help.

∽⌒∽

It says a lot about the gravity of Mike's condition that his concussion was considered the least of his problems. Because his lungs had ingested some sea water, he required an apparatus to help him breathe. The bacteria in the water had given him pneumonia and the weakened condition of his lungs meant he faced the risk of long-term infection. Complicating matters further was his wildly fluctuating blood pressure brought on by the trauma of the accident.

"Mike's immune system was very weak," says Beckie. "And one of the things I was extremely worried about was the way his blood pressure kept going up and down."

Mike appeared to be the one among them all who was least concerned about his immediate future. "I don't remember feeling any fear or panic," he would later observe. "I was just thankful to be alive." While he was medicated for the pain, Mike recalls understanding everything that was going on around him. Although his physical state was precarious, he felt alert and in good spirits.

Doug Cochrane relates that, despite everything else that was going on, the first thing Mike did during the hospital visit was turn to Barb to inquire about the construction of the Cochranes' summer place. "Here's this guy experiencing no lack of pain," says Cochrane, "and what you hear through the haze of a little bit of Demerol is, 'How's the building coming?'"

For Doug, and many others who know Mike, it was a typical Harcourt moment. "Mike doesn't tolerate fools," confides Cochrane. "He looks after himself and his family. But he has this interest in others that's very genuine. For him, it's always this attitude that carries the day. I guess the easiest way to describe him is that he sees the world as a cup half full rather than half empty."

Still, as Mike noted later, he couldn't help but notice that Doug looked worried and very pale. "It was all very nice that Mike was awake and could talk to us," explains Dr. Cochrane. "But the key question to me was, Can he do anything to control how his legs work? Would he be able to respond to a request from me?" So Doug inquired if his friend could move anything.

"Like what?" asked Mike.

"How about your left toe?" said Doug. Mike attempted to do as he was asked.

Beckie remembers the moment vividly. "The movement was so imperceptible that I couldn't really tell if Mike had moved anything," she says. "Neither could Michael, but Doug felt he saw it."

"He felt he did," Mike would later recall. "After that, I just saw this little smile come over his face."

∽∾∽

For the layperson, an almost imperceptible movement of the toe might not seem much to hang your hopes on. But for Dr. Cochrane it meant a great deal, both as a physician and, perhaps more importantly, as a devoted friend of the Harcourts. "My immediate response when I saw the toe move was tremendous relief," he explains, his voice breaking with emotion at the memory. "Even though the rest wasn't working very well, I thought, Thank goodness. This is wonderful."

Why did Dr. Cochrane respond so strongly to Mike having a whisper of voluntary movement in one toe? "The vast majority of people who have spinal cord injuries as a result of trauma lose their neurological function on a permanent basis," he explains. "One of the things that's a fair indication of whether that's going to be a permanent injury or not is if they have no control over a function that would have been served by the spinal cord below the level of their injury. That's when you know that things may not turn out so good.

"On the other hand, if you have someone who's able to voluntarily do something on command—for example, send a signal from their brain down to their big toe—it says that at least something's getting through. That's an entirely different indicator of prognosis... So it looked like the best of a bad thing. It looked as if nature had been good to Mike. I mean, it could have turned out very differently."

❧

The CT scan and MRI ultimately confirmed Dr. Cochrane's initial spark of hope. It was determined that Mike had an incomplete neck fracture—or more specifically a badly fractured mid-neck vertebrae—between the C6 and C7 level of the spine. Even though the fall had left him paralyzed in the legs and hands, the key word here is *incomplete*.

The good news was that Mike's injury had rendered him a partial quadriplegic, which left open the possibility he might ultimately regain significant movement in his legs. Again, it seemed Mike's luck was holding out, since statistics show that approximately 80 percent of people with similar injuries become complete quadriplegics, a condition that can mean life in a wheelchair because the spine is cut off from adequate communication with the brain below the level of injury.

The bad news was that Mike had what Dr. Dvorak calls "a high-energy injury"—the type of accident most commonly associated with car crashes or diving injuries. The doctor speculates that, in all likelihood, Mike landed on his head during the fall. The impact damaged a vertebrae and displaced a disc, which put pressure on the spine and altered the alignment of his spinal column. In addition, the bony fragments from the disc threatened to do further damage, raising the frightening possibility of severing the cord. An operation was essential if Mike was to have any hope of recovery.

Like many others involved in Mike's case, Dr. Dvorak says the possibility of getting him into surgery quickly made a huge difference. It doesn't always happen that way, particularly when the accident victim is in a lone vehicle at a remote location.

"That's one of the problems we face with people in other parts of the province," he explains. "People roll their cars and some of them aren't found until the next day. You know, someone's driving along and they notice these tire tracks heading off somewhere. The victim spends hours being extracted from the injury site. They're resuscitated, but they're hypothermic and near dead.

"After that, they face a six hour drive to the airport. But the airport doesn't have lights so they can't land at night. They have to wait until the next day to get to us." Dvorak shakes his head in wonderment. "Some of these stories..." he says. "It's just unbelievable that people survive."

Both Mike and Beckie knew they were extremely fortunate to have Dr. Dvorak on call at a major metropolitan hospital. "We were dealing with somebody who's done hundreds of operations," says Beckie. "That was a huge piece of luck right there."

Mike's proposed surgery would take approximately six hours. The operation involved multiple steps, including removing all traces of the fragmented disc; fusing and stabilizing the spine with pins and metal plates; and then taking some bone out of Mike's hip in order to reconstruct the damaged vertebrae.

Dr. Dvorak points out that the Harcourts had the option of waiting. In fact, years ago, it was considered standard procedure to wait before undergoing spinal surgery. While Dvorak didn't discourage this option, he believes even the smallest movement during that wait could have risked doing more damage to Mike's spine.

It was a lot of information for Mike to take in at a very sensitive time. But, whether in his personal life or in politics, Mike was used to making tough decisions. "It's always been a process," he says. "Listen, weigh the various pros and cons, and then make a decision. I think my legal training helped me not to get emotional about the situation. If you use good judgment, there's a certain amount of detachment you have to have too. You learn to be cool-headed.

"Some of the best advice I've ever given to others is to stand back and try to be objective," he adds. "Sure, it may be terrible what's happening, but you can't let your perspective get all screwy. This is a hard-nosed decision. You have to be able to eliminate the inconsequential and make it."

As Mike explains, his experience in making good decisions when there's a lot at stake served him well during the discussion of the operation. "I'd had sixty years of practice when it comes to overcoming a fear of the unknown," he says. "I've never been 100 percent sure of how something's going to turn out, but that's the thing about experience. Success tends to build on success and gives you a certain confidence. So all that makes it easier, not only to come to a decision but to prepare yourself to try and accept the outcome."

∽∾∾

For both Mike and Beckie, the decision to have the operation as quickly as possible marked the beginning of a strategy that Mike would come to call Plan B. Plan A was their old way of life, a life where they could take many things, both large and small, for granted. Plan B meant honing a set of skills and attitudes that would allow them to prevail over the exhausting complexities of what many health professionals simply referred to as "the spinal cord world."

Even though it proved an unsettling time, Beckie felt certain of one thing. Like Mike, she was determined to move forward without being hampered by negative thoughts. This would become the heart of Plan B, and, like everything else in their married life, they would ultimately shape that plan together.

"From the very first, I knew I didn't want to waste a single moment on regret," she confides. "I didn't want to think about yesterday or tomorrow. Just now." When her mind began to wander toward darker thoughts, she would remind herself that the heart of her marriage still remained intact. She wasn't a widow and Mike was going to get help from some people she would soon come to recognize as "highly skilled and deeply committed."

The feeling she remembers most is gratitude. "I never once felt that our life was over," she says. "But I quickly realized we were entering a different chapter. It was kind of like starting all over again really. We just knew—even if it turned out that Mike was going to be in a wheelchair—we were both alive, we were together, and we were going to pull through."

⌘

Despite an impressively steady series of medical advances in recent years, a significant part of the spinal cord world remains a mystery. It is a world that Dr. Marcel Dvorak is devoted to illuminating. But he readily admits that you can never fully predict the ultimate effect that a surgical procedure and rehabilitation will have on a patient. "I've had patients where I've been highly optimistic about a certain outcome and, for one reason or another, it doesn't turn out that way," he confesses. "We just don't know everything."

And yet Dr. Dvorak also feels that it's vitally important never to take hope away from a patient. As long as that hope is also balanced with an honest assessment of the person's likely potential for rehabilitation. The doctor believes that part of his job is to maintain that balance. The rewards, he says, are something he experiences every day. "I see so much grace and courage on the part of patients from every walk of life," he explains. "It's just an amazing thing."

The doctor notes that in recent years, it has become increasingly common to see patients around Mike's age with severe spinal cord injuries. Traditionally, the majority of spinal cord patients tended to be young males in their teens to mid-twenties. Now, as the doctor notes, there's a "second peak" among older people as they become used to leading a much more active lifestyle into their senior years, a trend that's been encouraged by the legendary appeal of BC's outdoors.

According to Dr. Dvorak, it is sometimes more difficult for older spinal patients to adapt to the sudden challenge of their injury. "A spinal cord injury in someone who's a bit older is a unique thing," he says. "Their rehab potential is very different from that of an athletic 16-year-old who can push himself up, whip around, and learn all these new things very quickly."

At this point, the doctor could not be certain that Mike wouldn't be confined to a wheelchair for the rest of his life. There were still so many questions. Would Mike make it through the risky surgery without further damage? And, if so, how would his battered body respond to rehab? Only time would tell. Mike would later articulate the strong element of uncertainty in his new world by saying, "The spinal cord gods are very capricious." He would often use this expression when people speculated too far into the future.

Asked about the risk factor in Mike's operation, Dr. Dvorak approaches the question from two different perspectives. "From a technical complexity point of view, Mike's type of operation is one that we do fairly frequently," he says. "So it's not like, say, separating Siamese twins. But I think from a risk point of view it's totally different. You have an injured spinal cord that's swollen and very susceptible to further damage. It's being squeezed by bone and these disc and bony fragments. In relieving that pressure—taking the pressure off and realigning the spine—the risk of making things worse even temporarily is fairly significant."

Dr. Dvorak points out that there's always a heightened risk when operating on the cervical spinal cord, including making the condition worse as a result of the surgery. "If someone with a C6–C7 injury ascends to a C5-6 injury, that's a huge difference," he explains. "There can be a risk of that if the spinal cord is unduly manipulated if, for example, that disc fragment is pushed back into the spinal canal when we're trying to realign the spine. That's been described in papers and surgical reports as causing dramatic worsening of spinal cord injuries."

But Dr. Dvorak also observes that cases such as Mike's have clearly benefited from medical advances during the last decade, both in terms of technology and surgical approach. Like Dr. Cochrane, he observes that "ten years ago, we probably wouldn't have had as good MRI images." He also points out that "we didn't know as much about how a pushed-back disc can cause worsening when we straighten the spine out."

In fact, a decade ago, the operation that would have been proposed to Mike would have been quite different. "What we probably would have done is put tongs on Mike's head and performed what's called a closed reduction," says Dvorak. "It's done by pulling and manipulating and getting things lined up again. There's a fairly significant chance that it could have made him worse."

ᢒᢙᢓᢙᢒ

In the end, the decision was simple. For Mike, going ahead with the operation amounted to putting his trust in two professionals whose judgment he valued. "I had Doug and Marcel, who were in basic agreement, so there was every reason to hope for the best," he explains. "I suppose I could have procrastinated. But why duck what has to be done? To me, that's a little like being in denial. I didn't feel any fear or any panic. I just figured this is what has to be done, so I didn't pause a bit."

Beckie agrees. "Neither of us hesitated," she says. "This is what was needed and we had to get prepared quickly. I remember them saying, 'The operating room's ready. We've got to go.'"

Thanks to the quick work of various health and rescue professionals, Mike would find himself on the operating table a mere ten hours after the accident. The last thing he remembers before the operation is looking at Marcel and telling him, "Go for it. And I hope to see you in the morning."

4

REGROUPING

"When you're going through hell, just keep on going."
— WINSTON CHURCHILL

Twenty-two-year-old Justen Harcourt was in an upbeat mood when he called his parents' North Pender Island number on Sunday, December 1, from Stockholm, intending to tell his mom and dad what a great time he was having. He was backpacking through Europe with a friend while waiting to hear if he'd been accepted to study at the London School of Economics. The trip was intended to serve as a break before he started his graduate studies in urban planning.

When no one answered at the cottage, Justen phoned the family's Vancouver number. It was around 9 A.M. Beckie was at home, waiting for her son's regular call.

"I knew immediately that something was wrong," he says. "It was just the tone in my mom's voice. She told me not to worry, but I had this terrible, gut-churning feeling hearing her describe what had happened. It was like the world had suddenly been flipped upside down."

Justen recalls sitting in the basement of his hostel and trying to absorb the full impact of his mother's news. "I just remember feeling completely numb and absolutely confused about what to do next," he says. "There was this complete loss of direction." He ended up going for an emotionally sobering walk with his friend Dave Kotler through the streets of Stockholm. It was the first snowfall of the year, but Justen barely noticed as the flakes drifted gently toward the ground. After explaining to Dave what had happened, Justen said he needed to go home.

For Justen, it wasn't the homecoming he had anticipated. "The next twenty-four hours of my life were the darkest and most painful of my life," he confides. "I kept picturing my father lying motionless in a hospital bed and having to cope with the trauma and the surgery. It was a long flight home."

⌘

The first stage of the operation began at about 11 P.M. on the Saturday, with Mike lying on the operating table face up. Dr. Dvorak made an incision in the front of his neck, removed the disc fragments, and performed the realignment procedure—the riskiest part of the operation. Once this was done, a bone graft was put in, along with a metal plate. This stage took up approximately two-thirds of the six-hour operation—a proportion that Dr. Dvorak explains is also roughly equivalent to the level of intensity and risk.

The second part of the operation was done with Mike lying face down. It involved using a special table that flipped him over while holding his neck in the correct position for surgery. Dr. Dvorak made an incision in the back of Mike's neck. He put in a small plate and some screws, then removed some of the bone from Mike's spine to create more room for the spinal cord. This second stage represented about one-third of the operation.

⌀⌀⌀

Beckie knew from the start that the operation would be long, so she drove home as it started to try to get some sleep. It was the first time she had been back to the family's Vancouver home since the accident, and the house seemed strangely quiet and empty. She got through some of the next six hours by trying to clear her mind and focus on her breathing. At other times, she would pray. "I remember praying for Michael to be alive," she confides. "I just prayed for hours."

Throughout those early morning hours, Beckie tried to stay positive. "Mike has always been a very lucky person," she says. "We've always realized that on some level because we've felt it in our own lives. When an accident like this happens, it's easy to think, Well, maybe our luck has run out. But when you see the very best medical people coming together for Mike's benefit, it makes you deeply grateful."

Still, those hours were among the most difficult of her ordeal. "When I came home that night, I just got under the covers and I started to shake," she recalls. "That would happen quite often during those first couple of weeks."

It was the beginning of a pattern that she would learn to cope with. "During the daytime, I'd be quite calm and quite focused on the things that needed to be done. But at night I'd have a great deal of trouble sleeping and I'd start to shake." When this happened, she would try to calm down by clearing her mind, breathing deeply, and drinking chamomile tea.

At 5 A.M., shortly after the operation was finished, an exhausted Beckie received a call from Marcel. She describes his tone as cautiously optimistic. Mike had made it through the operation in good spirits, he said, an attitude that Mike would need to maintain to get through the long and difficult weeks of post-operative care that lay ahead. In the hours following the operation, Mike would have some movement in one leg but no movement in the other. He would have good movement in his upper arms but none in his fingers.

As for Mike's mood, he recalls his spirits lifting as soon as he awoke from surgery. "The first thing I saw was Marcel with a couple of his kids in tow peering at me," says Mike. He laughs, adding, "I thought, I'm alive. This is a good sign. I wasn't depressed or in shock. I was just pleased to be alive and to see Marcel with his kids."

But Mike and Beckie didn't have much time to savour the surgery's success. With everything that was going on around them, many urgent things still needed to be resolved.

⌒⌒⌒

Barb Cochrane was waiting for Justen when he stepped off the plane. "She greeted me with the greatest, most reassuring hug I have ever had," he says. "More importantly, she told me that everything was going to be okay. It was like some great weight had been lifted off my shoulders."

For Beckie, Justen's homecoming helped her recover some measure of her daily routine. "I could start to focus on him and regular family things like getting groceries. So, on the one hand, there was our hospital life. And, on the other hand, there's everything you need to do to keep a household going. Having Justen around was just very helpful that way."

Justen's assistance over the coming months would also provide vital support for his parents—starting with a media conference, where he extended thanks to a concerned public on behalf of his parents, and continuing well into his dad's rehab process.

As Justen explains, he would draw strength from the constant example of his mother. "My mother has cared for my father more than any other person," he says. "Her strength and resolution has helped my father and me immensely. Her actions after dad's accident have shown us both what true love really means."

Justen confides that he's always been especially close to his parents—a bond that he partly attributes to the ups and downs of political life. "Growing up in a political family, where everybody wants something from you means there are times when you don't really know who your true friends are," he observes. "That makes for a closer relationship with the people that you really care about. I'm fiercely protective of my parents, as they are of me."

As Justen relates, he was exposed to the realities of public life at an early age. As a kid, he recalls how much fun it was hanging out with Mike in the mayor's office. "I learned how to make paper airplanes with my dad on the third floor of city hall," he recalls. "At the time, it seemed to me that he had the greatest job ever. I very quickly became aware of the reality of his career later in life. He didn't enter politics to become rich and powerful. He did so because it was the right thing to do, regardless of the personal sacrifice. What better role model do you need?

"My relationship with my parents has been continually tested and reforged as a result of my father's political career," he adds. "It was so constantly demanding that we had no one else to rely on except each other. I trust them and respect their perspective on life. It basically comes down to loyalty."

As caregivers, some difficult times lay ahead for both Beckie and Justen. They could not begin to anticipate the high levels of stress and anxiety they would experience during the coming months. But visiting

Mike in recovery after the operation was one of the many times they would feel a sense of renewal. "Seeing my father in the hospital was the greatest day of my life so far," says Justen. "Just seeing him alive was the best gift I've ever gotten. The whole thing was this amazing confirmation of how lucky I am to be his son. His approach to the situation was inspiring."

⌘

Typically, Mike recalls that he was eager to see how much movement he could recover as soon as possible. On the first post-op day, he says, "I was starting to do some soft therapy and they had me sitting up in this special chair. I thought it was a cup of tea."

On the second day, Mike was visited by Rick Hansen. "I said Mike this is a hell of a way to mount a political comeback," Hansen recalls. "Then of course in classic Mike fashion, he said, 'If you let anybody know about that, I'll tell them that you're running for the NDP.'"

A renowned activist for spinal cord research, Hansen had been in a motor vehicle accident that left him in a wheelchair at the age of fifteen. Mike, who has supported Rick's efforts to learn more about spinal cord injuries since his days in the mayor's office, talked to his friend about the possibility of taking on a new role as a spinal cord advocate.

Rick Hansen remembers that day well. "When I heard about Mike's injury, my first thought was that I really wanted to reach out to him and be there as a friend," says Rick. "We've had a long relationship, so I just wanted to come with an open heart and offer him my support."

And yet, despite his wish to buoy Mike's spirits, Hansen's knowledge of the turmoil surrounding spinal trauma left him feeling cautious. "I called and asked if he was up for a visit," he says. "You never know how people are feeling at the time. They could be in agonizing pain. Anybody who knows anything about this type of injury knows that it's really tough."

When Rick arrived in Mike's room, he was in for a surprise. "I was just blown away by his optimism and his sense of humour," says Hansen. "He's got all this stuff going on—he's hooked up to all the bells and whistles—and he's cracking jokes. You could tell he was in pain, but it wasn't the morphine talking. It was like he was trying to find something positive in the situation.

Hansen, who regularly visits people with spinal cord injuries, recalls gently probing beyond Mike's characteristic sense of humour and optimism. "You could tell that Mike had already spent a lot of time getting to understand the situation," he says. "He'd already formulated his battle plan."

As Rick discovered, part of Mike's battle plan was to find a way to help others through his own injury. "It was classic Mike," recalls Hansen. "He starts turning the tables and asking me what I've been up to, pumping me for information. The next thing I know, he says, 'Well, look, as soon as I get through this rehab process, come and meet me again. I want to know more about what you're doing because I want to help out.'"

Hansen was deeply affected by his friend's offer, given his traumatic circumstances. "I just went out of there going, 'Man, that's an amazing guy,'" Hansen says. "I learned about another layer of Mike. I guess I should have assumed it based on the level he had risen to in public life. But he demonstrated such grace in a very difficult situation."

Typically, Mike had gotten carried away with the enthusiasm of learning how he could turn his situation into something positive. When Hansen left, Mike had been sitting upright in his chair for close to five hours. But even the pain of remaining in the same position for too long served as a valuable lesson.

"It was just too much," says Mike. "I really overdid it and I could feel the effects afterwards. It was the first time I realized that if I was going to get through all this I was going to have to pace myself."

Dr. Dvorak recalls that second day after Mike's surgery. "He was a little down. He felt kind of beat-up and he had sat for a little too long. His pneumonia was a little worse that day and he hadn't slept very well the night before, so everything was sort of catching up with him."

Beckie remembers those early days at VGH as being especially exhausting for her husband. "Michael had always been this super-healthy star," she says. "And when he became bedridden and so ill, it was a different kind of challenge. He'd never had to deal with his body to that degree before, so I think making that adjustment was one of the tougher parts of the journey for him."

༚

Mike would be spending three weeks at VGH. His surroundings weren't exactly cheerful, but it never occurred to him to request a private room. "I never even thought about it," he says. "I just figured that I was going to go through this like anybody else." In the process, he would be exposed to situations that would repeatedly drive home the heartbreak associated with spinal trauma.

"There was a fellow who was in there who had an infection from a drug injection," Mike recalls. "His spine was infected and he was moaning and swearing terribly because he had developed a tolerance for the morphine and they couldn't give him enough to cope with the pain.

"Two young people came in, one right after the other," he adds. "Both had been in motor vehicle accidents and both were going to be paraplegics. There was a young guy who'd been airlifted from Victoria and a young girl who was seeing demons and crying for her dad. She was in terrible pain. You could just feel the two of them and their families trying to come to grips with it all. It was hard."

While all this was happening, Mike was being continually examined in the wake of his surgery. The tests included additional X-rays and the constant monitoring of his lung capacity and erratic blood pressure. "There was just a lot happening around me," he recalls. "Doctors, technicians, and all kinds of specialists coming in. All kinds of pills that I had to take, and all this tragedy going on around me."

                                     ∽✖∾

It was during this second day after the operation that the reality of Mike's situation finally took hold. That afternoon, he hit his lowest point emotionally. "It suddenly occurred to me that I was going to be changed forever, however well I recovered," he says. "It was a horrifically different set of circumstances from what I was used to. It wasn't one specific fear, just realizing that there was a whole range of things that I was going to have to face. It just sunk in that my paralysis was very real."

Mike's sense of panic lasted only for a minute or so before he managed to cut his negative feelings short. "I kind of gave myself an emotional slap in the face," he confides. "I remember thinking, Okay, Harcourt, get over it. Plan A is over. It's time to get on with Plan B. I was alive and I had some movement, so I just decided I was going to go right at recovery."

Mike recalls getting inspired by Roy Jenkins' biography of Winston Churchill, which a friend gave him to read in the hospital. One of Churchill's sayings from his experiences in the Second World War struck Mike as particularly apt to his own situation: "When you're going through hell, just keep on going."

For Mike, focusing on moving forward fit his personality. "I never liked to put in a lot of time brooding about things before the accident," he says. "No matter how complex the process is, I don't like to second-guess things after I've integrated them intellectually and emotionally. It's just not in my nature to torture myself with dark thoughts or regrets."

It also helped that Mike has always been a positive person. "A sense of optimism has been so deeply engrained in me for so long that it was nothing new," he says. "It wasn't as though I was suddenly inspired to be optimistic after the accident. It just made sense to me not to ponder too much about how my life had changed because it already had, so why worry about it?"

Mike also points out that, at sixty, he'd already gotten the message that life has its unexpected ups and downs no matter how hard you try to avoid them. His lifelong sense of humour combined with a philosophical attitude about the nature of fate.

"I've always had this theory that everybody's crazy," he says with a laugh. "Life is so tough that you already have to be crazy to be alive. I mean that in the best sense. We've all got deep fears and uncertainties," he adds. "Questions like, How did I get here in the universe? and Is there a God? You could have a bolt of lightning strike you under a tree or get caught in an earthquake. Who knows? You just have to do the best you can with what you've got."

From that moment on, the goal of Plan B was clear. "I wanted to get myself in shape and have as high a quality of life as possible," he explains. "For myself, for Beckie, for Justen, and for all the issues that I wanted to remain engaged in.

"In a way, it was nothing new," he says, of his ability to regroup so quickly. "I had to pull myself up a few times like that during my political life, plus I've had a lot of practice at setting long-term and short-term goals, not just for me, but also in terms of figuring out where my city should go, or my province.

"So I had practice in facing a number of different challenges. That's important because, while I've sometimes had to make certain adjustments, there have also been times when I've been surprised by the level of my success."

For Mike, facing the greatest challenge of his life meant remaining as open to the possibility of success as always. "It was like, Okay, it's time to do this again," he observes. "Only this time, I knew I had to recreate the essence of what was important to me from the perspective of someone with a spinal cord injury."

∽✴✲

Mike found that getting a close look at other people's predicaments gave him a valuable perspective on his own situation. "I was a partial quad," he says. "And, while there were no guarantees that I would have the full use of my hands and legs again, I was being exposed to these people who were complete paraplegics.

They were so young and the lives they had known previously were suddenly trashed.

"If you're in your twenties, you often work under the assumption that you're immortal," Mike adds. "You tend to think of life as having no limits, that it's just going to be a bowl of cherries with the perfect job and the perfect relationship. Then, all of a sudden, you have a skateboarding accident or a diving accident and everything goes awry."

Mike also quickly realized that the bizarre story behind his own injury was not an isolated case. "There was a young woman who was camping with her boyfriend," he says. "She's standing by the tent and he's getting ready to build a fire. The boyfriend is bent down to get some wood for the fire. The next time he looks up, she's gone. She'd stepped back over a fifty-foot cliff. Now she's in an electric wheelchair and her life is suddenly totally transformed. Stories like those just made me realize that there were so many others who were worse off."

Similar insights weren't lost on Beckie or Justen, who would visit Mike three or four times a day at VGH. "Every time we saw each other we were provided with this very clear perspective on all the people in the ward," explains Beckie. "Each time, we were reminded that Mike was mentally healthy and he wasn't experiencing the kind of terrible pain that some people were going through."

Beckie observes that Mike's lack of chronic pain made a huge difference to the family's outlook from the start. "We were very grateful that Mike didn't have to deal with the issue of constant pain," she says. "Since he wouldn't have to deal with finding the right combination of painkillers, his mind was always very clear, so he could make a lot of decisions as they came along."

Justen points out that Mike's mental attitude has consistently been a key factor in his dad's success. His father's determination—at a time when he needed it the most—was simply an extension of the way he had always been.

⌇⌇⌇

"The day after my return was the start of my new life as the son of the greatest man I've ever known," Justen remarks. "I know he says he only had one dark moment before he decided that it was on to Plan B. But I'm positive that he had all sorts of questions running through his head, just as I had all sorts of questions running through mine about why this had happened to him. Politics was easy in comparison to his trials and tribulations as a recovering spinal cord patient."

And yet, for Justen, these possible doubts were less important than how his father coped with them. "He chose to work hard at regaining his abilities, even though there was no guarantee that he would walk again," he says. "The percentage of even a marginal recovery was small, but he wasn't going to feel sorry for himself. He was just going to try and rebuild his life and move on from there.

"Sometimes the only thing you can do in life is focus on where you want to get to by taking one painful step at a time," Justen continues. "I knew my dad would use every ounce of his energy to recover. But I also knew that his energy would be strengthened by the faith he had in himself." The fundamental values of having faith in himself and facing challenges one step at a time underlie Mike's approach to life, Justen added.

Beckie agrees. "Setting goals has always been an extremely strong motivator for Mike," she says. "So even though he could hardly move at all and he was very ill because of the infection in his lungs, I knew as soon as he realized, Hey, I'm alive that he would be clear on the message."

Dr. Dvorak recalls that Mike's response to his situation seemed unusually upbeat. "I remember I kept waiting for the crash because sometimes there's a crash—or at least a dip. But it never really happened to any extent. That's just the kind of guy Mike is. I really don't know whether I'd be that way under the same circumstances."

∽⌒∾

Part of the reason Mike remained in good spirits was the immediate feeling that his lifelong advocacy for the disabled could benefit both the hospital and fellow spinal patients. If his advocacy had now taken a deeply personal turn, well, so much the better. Mike put it this way: "As long as this has happened to me, I might as well take advantage of it by doing some good."

"He talked about how maybe this wasn't such a terrible thing," says Dr. Dvorak, of Mike's first words after they removed his breathing tube. "That maybe he'd be able to help others because of it. I mean this was the first thing he said. They took the tube out of his mouth and he's already talking about where we can go with this. I find that absolutely remarkable."

Both Beckie and Justen consider this attitude typical of Mike. They point out that one of his heroes was Tommy Douglas, the father of Canadian medicare. In fact, one of Mike's favourite Douglas quotes is, "What we want for ourselves, we want for others." He has always tried to work that philosophy into all aspects of his life, even in the face of great personal change.

"He really thinks bigger than himself, which is an amazing influence," says Justen. "His priorities are not just himself and his family, but also his city, his province, and his country. His thought process is so completely different from anyone else I know because it always includes a vision about what we should be doing as a society and how we should get there."

Mike notes that his age at the time of the accident gave him an advantage, both in terms of coping with his own circumstances and looking at the bigger picture. "You can't help but accumulate a certain amount of knowledge and experience as you get older," he says. "It really helps you deal more effectively with unexpected change. Plus, I had accomplished a lot of the things I'd set out to do at the time of my injury. I've lived well, so it's a bit easier not to feel bitter and rejected."

∽∾∾

Many of Dr. Dvorak's patients lack the benefit of Mike's life experience. The majority are young, active males whose lives will be drastically changed by their spinal injury whether they end up in a wheelchair or not. Some naturally meet the challenge of their new circumstances with the same tenacity they brought to life before the accident.

Marcel recalls operating on a young man who was severely injured in a snowboarding accident. "He was kind of a shredder," says the doctor affectionately. "But you just knew he was going to be alright—that he was going to approach his rehab with a unique kind of spirit." And yet for other patients, coping with a serious spinal injury is much more difficult. "It may seem odd, but some of my most depressed patients are the ones who have the greatest recovery," Marcel adds. "They come back and I say, 'Look at that! You've walked into the clinic. This is fantastic.' However, even though they're doing very well, they still have to deal with a profound disability and all the problems that go along with that. They're able to walk, but are they able to walk quickly?" he asks. "They don't have the push-off strength in their feet, so while they're able to walk very slowly down the hall, they may not be able to go for a walk with their girlfriend or keep up with somebody they meet on the street."

"Things like bowel and bladder function will never be the same," he adds. "It will require more attention, more care, more everything."I had one 23-year-old guy break down in tears," he recalls. "He told me he couldn't go into a bar because, if he drinks a beer, he'll pee himself. And, if he meets a girl, his sexual function isn't normal. This is someone who's profoundly lonely and near suicidal. And yet everyone's slapping him on the back and telling him how lucky he is not to be in a wheelchair. I know a lot of my patients get tired of hearing that because every single one of them is living with a major disability," he says. "We just don't recognize it or measure it properly."

And yet, thanks to the intense media coverage of Mike's injury, that lack of recognition would change.

One of the first things Mike did during the early phase of his recovery was commit to a seven-part series in the *Vancouver Sun* by reporter Lori Culbert. Entitled *The Road Back*, it would draw attention to the unique needs of the spinal cord world by focusing on the various stages of Mike's recovery.

It was a risky move, considering that nobody knew just how well Mike would do in rehab, but he was determined to show that the health care system works—despite the improvements needed in it. What better way to draw attention to the dedication of various health professionals than to chronicle his progress? And with the media showing Mike a level of concern and affection that one reporter accurately described as phenomenal, there was no better time to shed some much-needed light on the rehabilitation process.

From the start, Mike's accident was the lead story on both national and regional newscasts for days. Prime Minister Jean Chrétien phoned several times to offer his best wishes. "He was wonderfully warm and supportive," recalls Mike. Former Prime Minister Brian Mulroney called twice. Friends, strangers, and politicians of all stripes were united in their heartfelt concern for Mike's welfare. One of the gifts that Mike found especially touching was a rugby ball autographed by the same members of the local media he had dubbed "the scrum of the earth" during his days in provincial politics.

The outpouring of goodwill not only crossed political, social, and media boundaries but actually helped unite an often divided British Columbia in a common cause. His long-time friend, veteran talk-show host Vicki Gabereau put the feeling best when she said, "The entire province—indeed the entire country—just held their breath."

For Mike, the massive amount of public support clearly proved inspiring. "So many people were saying prayers at Sikh temples and Jewish synagogues and Catholic masses," he recalls. While Mike doesn't consider himself religious in the traditional sense, the support from people of various faiths reinforced the all-encompassing nature of his spirituality. "In a sense, the accident has worked to expand on my Christian upbringing," he confides. "I feel like all religions are valid. Whatever path you take—whether you're a Christian, Muslim, or Jew—they flow into that one creation."

The compassion he received from so many different people had a positive effect on Mike's disposition. "It was terrific because you're sort of floating along on this encouragement," he says. "It was very moving and the whole thing just sort of fed into my motivation."

"It was a huge outpouring of love," adds Beckie. "Michael and I both felt it very strongly. People were just so kind to us." Both Mike and Beckie were over-whelmed by the wave of concern—a wave that has shown no sign of abating since the day of the accident. The Harcourts find themselves at a loss to explain such a strong and lasting response, but to their family, friends, and colleagues, it has everything to do with their basic approach to life. As Beckie says, "We've lived the values we've espoused."

Part of Mike's popularity stems from his ability to separate a person's political views from his or her qualities as a person. "Who someone is as a human being is far more important than what their political biases are," he says. "This is particularly true in a province like British Columbia. If you only saw people with the same political values, you'd cut off half the population right off the bat."

His political philosophy, like his personal life, has always been straightforward. He was competitive but fair. When it came to crossing swords behind the closed doors of political back rooms, he let his ethics guide him. "I was never prepared to get down and dirty," he says. "Nineteen times out of twenty, I've found that you can reach a consensus with people. But when things got heavy, I was always very tough-minded. Chances are I would win and the other guy wouldn't." "I've had to make some difficult decisions," says Mike of his political career. "I've had to be tough-minded, focused, and willing to accept the consequences of my actions, but that doesn't mean you have to be mean-spirited or vindictive about it."

His approach reflects his belief that nice guys can finish first. "This idea that you have to be a ruthless bully to be successful is nonsense," he says. "I don't think most people operate that way. Some people get away with that for a while, but it'll catch up with them. You're far better off playing it straight and up front with people and treating them with respect and decency."

❧

As Dr. Don Williams explains, Mike's beliefs had an effect on people across Canada. He recalls feeling deeply touched by the public's heartfelt concern for Mike in the aftermath of his accident. "I can't believe the reaction," Williams says. "I've had people come up to me and pat me on the back. They say things like, 'Thank you so much.' This is all over BC in little, tiny towns, but the response is the same when I travel back east. I think there's something about the way Mike has lived his life," he continues. "People really do feel connected to him. Maybe they don't realize how strongly they make those connections in so many different ways, but they do."

Dr. Williams explains this connection by observing that Mike's optimistic outlook offers hope to people from all walks of life. He recalls his first visit to Mike at VGH. "Mike made it into this wonderful experience," says Williams. "He kept telling me how great the nurses were and how he was going to beat this thing. He was just putting this tremendously positive spin on everything."

Dozens of articles and magazine pieces from across the country would emerge in the months that followed, many attempting to analyze why people were so genuinely moved by Mike's situation. Perhaps the piece that explained the outpouring of affection best was written by *Globe and Mail* columnist Michael Valpy not long after the accident. Valpy—a boyhood pal of Mike's from their days on a church basketball team—described himself as a perpetual benchwarmer, who saw almost no game time. He writes of how Mike, whom he calls "a magician on the court," insisted that Valpy play in the closing minutes of an important game. "I've talked to the coach," said Mike. "We're going into the game together."

"That moment has stayed in my memory," writes Valpy. He goes on to explain that his friend has been a kind and decent human being "for as long as anyone has known him." It would seem that years before Mike met Tommy Douglas he was finding different ways to share the joy of his own dreams and goals with others.

It's the kind of thing that people tend to remember. And many of them chose to express their memories in different ways.

The Vancouver Museum started a book of greetings that made it possible for everyone to convey their feelings. The book was filled with get-well wishes from locals who had encountered Mike on the street or at the supermarket. One note was from a man who used to fill Mike's car with gas. "You always took the time to say hello," it said.

So many flowers came in from well-wishers across the country that Mike and Beckie distributed them throughout the hospital. Cards poured in from Mike's long list of friends and acquaintances.

〜∽〜

Two of Mike's favourite cards provided both solace and inspiration, mirroring his efforts to balance the serenity that came from accepting his fate with the tenacity that he would need to make the most of his recovery.

One card featured a Buddhist saying:

When we understand

things are just as they are.

When we don't understand,

things are just as they are.

The other card featured a quote from Muhammad Ali. It read: "Champions aren't made in gyms. Champions are made from something they have deep inside them—a desire, a dream, a vision. They have to have the skill and the will. But the will must be stronger than the skill."

Granted, there were times when the competitive streak in Mike seemed much more like Ali on the comeback trail than your typical Buddhist. Consider that, while still at VGH, he continued to fulfill his commitments as a board member for both the Vancouver Port Authority and the Vancouver International Airport, attending meetings via telephone conferences. As vice-chair of the cities^{PLUS} project—and part of a Vancouver-based team that was gearing up for an international competition to chart the best future for sustainable cities—Mike was regularly on the phone ironing out details and making sure his colleagues met various deadlines.

For Mike, remaining engaged in these projects a mere week after his accident was a crucial part of his overall recovery. After more than thirty years of marriage to Mike, Beckie understood what was going on. "At that point, about the only thing that was really functioning fully in Mike was his mind," she remarks. "So he really needed an outlet for it." Others were taken aback by Mike's constant drive to get his life back in order.

"There was this psychologist," says Mike smiling. "She got so fed up with me. She thought I was getting kind of manic. She threatened me with a psychiatrist." He chuckles and adds, "I finally told her, 'Listen, you can bring in a psychiatrist if you want, but I'm just going to drive them crazy. So you better get used to the way I've decided to do this.'"

93

⌒⌒⌒

Always willing to be flexible, Mike agreed to a compromise with the psychologist and the rest of his doctors. He told them that as his health improved with each passing month he would devote an increasing amount of time to interests outside his therapy regime. "In December, I would channel 90 percent of my time into getting better and 10 percent into other things," he explains. "In January, it would be 80–20 and, in February, 70–30."

Asked what would happen after February, Mike smiles. "After that," he says. "I told them we'd negotiate."

Mike's negotiations reflected his sense of optimism as well as his constant desire to move forward. And yet, after two weeks at VGH, the movement in his limbs was still severely limited and a variety of infections would continue to wreak havoc on his immune system. In addition, he was still adjusting to the use of a catheter. As he moved into the G. F. Strong Rehabilitation Centre in mid-December, he was about to face his toughest challenge yet—a gruelling regime of physical and occupational therapy that would help determine if he would ever walk again.

5

STANDING UP AND STANDING OUT

"Every once in a while we get clients coming through who really spice up the floor. There's just this increase in energy—this hum of activity when they're out and about. Mike was definitely one of those guys. He built up a lot of camaraderie that clients could relate to, regardless of age or injury level."
— OCCUPATIONAL THERAPIST ROB GIACHINO

Rehabilitation was a process that Mike would compare to climbing a mountain. "I had to keep reminding myself that there were many different paths to the top," he says of the seemingly countless tasks he had to relearn. At times, he says, they seemed endless.

The mountain was of Everest proportions when Mike first arrived at the G. F. Strong Rehabilitation Centre, the largest rehab centre in British Columbia. His injury had left him virtually helpless, robbing him of the basic skills able-bodied people learn to take for

95

granted. Movement of any kind—even turning over in bed—was a major undertaking. His independence was curtailed by the fact that he was unable to get out of bed and into his wheelchair without someone placing him in the chair. Because of numbness in both hands, and a particular weakness in his dominant right hand, he was also unable to feed himself adequately, dress himself, or attend to his own toilet habits—a messy ritual that included getting used to a catheter.

As if all this wasn't enough to cope with, Mike had fallen victim to an extremely powerful bacterium during his stay at VGH. Known as *Clostridium difficile* or *C. difficile,* the bacterium resists virtually all antibiotics. It forms a toxin in the stomach and drains the body's energy through rampant diarrhea. Not only can *C. difficile* damage the colon, it's also potentially lethal. In fact, the bacteria has killed more people than SARS.

"It was sort of a ticking time bomb," says Mike of the infection. "If your bladder gets blocked, it can lead to an infection that backs up into your system and it can really be very serious."

಼ಾ಼

Mike's ongoing bladder and bowel problems made him especially grateful to the nurses who took care of him, both at G. F. Strong and previously at the Vancouver General Hospital. "They were terrific," he remarks. "They did all the dirty work and all the messy stuff from changing my catheter to making sure I shifted position every few hours so that I wouldn't get bedsores. They were always cheerful and upbeat."

The nurses' attitude helped put Mike more at ease, despite the gravity of his situation. "There was the constant concern that the antibiotics wouldn't work," he says. "I remember a kind of floating uncertainty about it because I was never quite sure whether I'd be cured."

There was nothing to do except try to move forward despite the havoc various infections wreaked on Mike's system. He estimates that his constant bowel and bladder infections, combined with the draining effect of various antibiotics utilized to fight the worrisome onslaught of *C. difficile*, sapped about 75 percent of his energy. Consider that, in the short time since his accident, Mike had lost more than thirty pounds. "Food goes into your system and right out again," he says. "I would get really exhausted by the bug. I had to constantly battle through infections."

Despite his weakened state, Mike was able to go home briefly for Christmas. He was only there for a few hours, but his visit meant a lot to the Harcourt family. For Beckie it was especially meaningful to have Mike back in his home environment, if only to celebrate the familiar rituals of Christmas. However, she had mixed feelings about Mike being away from the hospital environment so soon.

"It was a good sign that he wanted to come home so badly," she recalls. "It showed that he was getting better." But Beckie adds that it was also a traumatic time for her. "I was worried sick about his blood pressure," she remembers. As always, her concerns gave way to a greater feeling that it was important for Mike to keep moving forward.

In a statement issued to reporters, Mike referred to the holiday as a welcome opportunity to celebrate a new chance at life with his family and friends. After the organized chaos of hospital life, he enjoyed the serenity of gazing out his own living room window at the view of the city and the mountains. Later, he would call the holiday the most meaningful of his entire life.

On Christmas day—as he had done every day since the accident—Mike would pray. He did so twice daily, upon waking up and before going to sleep. The prayer was a brief but important bookend to his day that would help get him through the trials of rehab. A simple way to give thanks for what he considered the greatest gift of all. The gift of being alive. The Harcourts would have eight people over for Christmas dinner and Mike would return to the hospital that evening. But he had proved that despite his ill health he could regain an important part of his family routine.

After Christmas, Mike would settle into the routine of rehab. It was natural to focus on whether he would be able to walk away from life in a wheelchair. Still, there were many other vital aspects of his rehabilitation to consider. G. F. Strong would be his home for close to three months as he tried to relearn fundamental life skills from the perspective of a partial quadriplegic.

Mike would jokingly refer to his time at the rehab clinic as boot camp. But as he adapted from the acute care at VGH to the demands of daily therapy at G. F. Strong, he knew he needed to shift into a higher gear. "It's the difference between tender, loving care and tough love," he says, explaining the philosophy of the two facilities. "But I needed to be taught the basics for getting back to an independent life."

A team of physicians, therapists, and health-care workers would provide crucial advice and assistance. It was led by Dr. Andrea Townson, medical manager of the spinal-cord-injury rehab program at G. F. Strong and a specialist in physical medicine and rehabilitation, who typically sees patients from the first days of their injury all the way through to their integration back into the community. The team's other members included veteran physiotherapist Maura Whittaker, occupational therapist Rob Giachino, and nurses Chris Clark and Colleen Powers.

As Dr. Townson explains, one of the team's primary goals for Mike was making sure that its members continued to document his neuralgic progress in order to set realistic goals for his rehabilitation. In order to determine these goals a number of issues must be considered, ranging from infections to pressure sores and bladder and bowel control. In the past, it was common to have quite a bit of time between hospital care and the beginning of rehab. But, in accordance with the current way of thinking, Mike's therapy would begin as soon as possible. There was no time to waste if they were going to maximize the possibility of Mike's recovery.

"For the first five or six weeks, I was getting out of the extreme paralysis state and getting the muscles stimulated and reacting again," says Mike. "So it wasn't like I could just grit my teeth through it. I knew it was going to be very tough to get through and it was. Every minute was a challenge."

Mike had many medical problems. But the philosophy of G. F. Strong is designed to co-ordinate the various skills of the rehab team skills so that the patient gets a clear picture of where he is in the process at all times. "Different team members may be working on similar goals in a complementary way," explains Dr. Townson, of the clinic's integrated style. "So, while the occupational therapist and the physiotherapist will be working toward different aspects of the same common goal, it's very much a team approach."

Dr. Townson stresses that the patient is "the first and foremost member of that team." As such, Mike's wishes were taken into consideration as much as possible. "We're there to provide the expertise to say, 'This is what we can do. How do you want us to try and do it?'" she says. As always, however, the limitations that stemmed from Mike's state of partial paralysis had to be factored into the equation.

While the members of Mike's health-care team emphasized that he was in the top 5 percent of the patients they see in terms of his potential for overall recovery, they initially predicted that his chances of recovering enough to walk again were approximately 50–50. They couldn't say whether he would walk without crutches or braces, if he was lucky enough to stand on his own two feet again.

Occupational therapist Rob Giachino puts it plainly. "The spinal cord's the boss," he says. "We're going to promote what we can and really get involved, but we can't do anything the spinal cord won't let us do."

At the same time, Mike immediately understood that nothing could change without a huge effort on his part. Because he had to relearn so many things, it was an effort that would begin from the moment he opened his eyes in the morning. "It's hard work from the minute you wake up," he explains. "Having to do the bowel and bladder thing and then having to do your toiletries in a wheelchair. Everything presents a new challenge, from shaving to eating your breakfast, where there would be utensils that I couldn't pick up."

Even getting from his second-floor bedroom down to rehab on the main floor initially proved a challenge. "You have to wheel your chair through these long hallways," he says. "When you're feeling sick anyway, that can be a very frustrating and tiring process." Of course the big question on everybody's mind was whether

Mike would be developing his wheelchair skills for permanent use.

"All clients come in overwhelmed and unsure of the future," says Rob. "But we had some hope for Mike because he had a lot of things going for him. We knew he'd be successful on certain levels. We just couldn't be certain that the success would include walking."

Still, Mike's injury was partial, and while some people would have been content with roughly even odds of walking out of G. F. Strong, he figured he could swing things in his favour with the right team and a proper attitude. In doing so, he would draw on his lifelong strength as a politician. His thinking? "Get the best people and go for it."

ᖇᕼᕯ

"I asked for the toughest and most demanding therapist and I got her," Mike says of physiotherapist Maura Whittaker. What he didn't know was that the woman he would affectionately dub "Major-General Maura" had actually requested his case.

Whittaker felt Mike's partial paralysis made him a good candidate for a potentially beneficial form of therapy known as functional electrical stimulation, or FES. A particular interest of Whittaker's, the therapy involves using a low level of electrical current to stimulate feedback between the spinal cord and the brain. A small box is strapped on to the patient and the electrical stimulation is started by turning on a switch. During therapy, the interval between electrical impulses is controlled with a timer. In use for the last decade or so, FES can stimulate nerves and cause repetitive movement in a specific joint such as the knee or ankle, an action that Mike was unable to perform on his own.

At the time, some negative articles in the press speculated that Mike might never get out of his wheelchair. Maura, a physiotherapist with more than twenty years of experience, believed she could help get Mike to maximize his potential for rehabilitation. It was a good match from the start.

"In no way have I accomplished the miraculous things that he's done," she says with the lilt of her native Ireland. "But there was definitely a meeting of the minds. Like Mike, I'm a problem-solver. I've pretty much seen it all—a huge variety of injuries—and he needed somebody like that."

"I knew we had a window of opportunity for Mike's injury," she continues. "But the really great part was how well Mike responded to the approach that there was no time to waste. He understood that we had to get going if we were to improve his overall function."

In Rob Giachino, Mike observes that he got "a really good, really focused occupational therapist." An enthusiastic young man, whose talents also included the kind of patience that all good therapists require, Rob would tell Mike that getting a decent shot at walking again was like building a house from the ground up. Fortunately, Mike felt ready to give his all toward building the proper foundation. "One of the first things you learn is that you can't walk unless your body is fully capable of supporting you," explains Mike. "And getting to that point takes a lot of very intense physiotherapy."

✂︎

For many patients, the rehabilitation process is the point where their new limitations hit them the hardest. But as Dr. Townson remarks, Mike's perspective, combined with the partial nature of his injury, would give him a fighting chance to achieve his objective of walking again. "Mike has an incredibly positive attitude," she says. "Having that attitude won't make you recover. But it will help you get the most out of any recovery you're going to have, and Mike was definitely determined to make the most of it."

In fact, Mike felt eager to set goals that would maximize his rehab and get him home as rapidly as possible. Part of the rehab team's job was taking Mike's personal needs into account, including his ongoing commitment to social issues. From Mike's perspective, continuing to fulfill his professional obligations on various boards and committees remained a vital part of the therapy process.

"Mike is a very caring individual who's highly involved in his community," says Dr. Townson. "The most challenging part for me was making sure that there was a balance between what he needed to do for rehabilitation and the demands in other aspects of his life."

Typically, Mike approached rehab in the same way he had approached life before his injury. "I was going to take on a double dose of therapy," he says. "I wanted out of G. F. Strong as quickly and with as much function as possible." His objective would encompass a gruelling regime that included up to four hours of physical therapy a day and at least one hour of occupational therapy.

"It's a real dynamic position to find yourself in," says Rob, of helping a patient make the right kind of choices. "Their world is torn apart, and they have no control and no say over that. They're looking at their life through a different lens. We have to help them make the transition to the realization that it's still their life and they have the final say."

As Maura Whittaker notes, the workload suited Mike's personality. "Mike was working at a hundred miles an hour and he didn't want to change," she says. "He didn't put himself in bed for a day if he wasn't feeling well. He was always up."

Mike set himself a strict deadline for leaving the G. F. Strong Centre. It was a demanding schedule, even for someone who was used to taking on a great deal of responsibility in his professional life. If everything worked out, he hoped to leave G. F. Strong in approximately half the normal time. But, just as importantly, Mike wanted to leave having achieved one very important task. Leaving behind his wheelchair and walking out of G. F. Strong by the end of February, a mere two and a half months away.

Mike talked openly to the media about his February 28 target date. It was part of a personal strategy to increase his motivation. "I kind of set myself up," he admits. "But, for me, it created an extra incentive."

There was also talk of shutting down G. F. Strong as part of government cutbacks. Revealing his recovery process to the media provided a way to shed light on how many dedicated people it takes to foster successful rehabilitation. "I wanted to make the point that there were a lot of talented people involved in the process. I felt it was important to get their story out."

Mike would rely on the talents of the G.F. Strong team to get him through many difficult times. One of the things that Mike had to do in rehab was push through genuine discomfort, including a sharp pain in his shoulder that would nag him throughout the initial stages of therapy. "The pain in my shoulder got very intense one time and I just stopped because I got dizzy," he recalls. "My blood pressure just dropped and I had to go back in my wheelchair."

And yet, despite the pain and his commitment to carrying on with various outside interests during his stay at G. F. Strong, Mike never missed a single therapy session, not only because of the sessions' importance but also because the regime was something the athlete in Mike could relate to.

"Michael was way better psychologically during therapy," Beckie confides. "I think it was because all that energy that had to be contained in his mind suddenly had a physical dimension. This was someone who was used to working ninety hours a week. Now all that drive was being totally focused on pulling together as much of his poor, broken body as he could."

Mike agrees. "For me, the physical part was the easiest part of the process in some ways," he explains. "I'm used to working out and pushing my boundaries. It was almost like getting in shape for an election or basketball season. So while it was exhausting and strenuous, at least I could focus on *doing*.

"You hear people talking about going into the zone in sports," Mike adds. "That's what I do. It's all part of the focus and the clarity I have about where I want to get to, whether it's settling treaties or working on sustainable cities or going through rehab."

❦

Doug Cochrane remembers visiting Mike shortly after he made the transition to G. F. Strong. As Dr. Cochrane observes, a simple stroll through the clinic's lobby will illustrate the different ways people deal with spinal cord injuries. "You can see the agony of the situation on a lot of people's faces," he says. "Partly, I think that stems from an inability to translate where they are to where they need to go. That's not something I apply to Mike at all. He's highly competitive, and this is something where he was competing."

And yet Doug also noticed that his friend was rapidly coming to a greater understanding of his situation. "It was clear that he had gotten through the early stages of a life-altering event," he explains. "That he really was going to focus on looking at his glass as half full."

For Mike, the choice of going into rehab was simple. "I think in this situation you have two basic options," he says. "You can be angry with the world, wallow in self-pity, and refuse to let go of Plan A. Or you can be positive and get on with Plan B. I chose to be positive."

Part of Mike's strategy for remaining upbeat consisted of constantly reminding himself how lucky he was. Like Beckie and Justen, he felt extremely grateful for the many obstacles that weren't in the way of his objectives. "I wasn't on a ventilator, for example," he notes. "And I was constantly seeing people who were worse off than me, people who were exhibiting tremendous grace and courage. They were determined to rebuild their lives, even though a lot of original expectations for life had been shattered."

Not that Mike didn't have his work cut out for him. According to Maura Whittaker, a number of uncertain variables had to be considered in Mike's case. "Because Mike's injury was partial, you're going to expect some neurological improvement," she explains. "But you don't know *how* neurological recovery is going to happen and you can never put money on what's going to come back and what's not. Walking or pulling yourself up may be impossible because you may only be able to do it on a partial basis."

～～～

On the plus side, Mike was responding positively to Maura Whittaker's use of functional electrical stimulation. During his first month of rehabilitation, Mike would receive one hour of FES per day.

"Research is now starting to show that electrical stimulation can actually cause changes in the brain," Maura explains. "Before they thought, 'Well, if something's happened that's it. There isn't a lot of capacity for recovery.' But that whole mindset is changing."

Since Mike's paralysis was incomplete, Whittaker felt he would benefit from electrical stimulation at various points on his weaker right side. It could help to get his neurons firing and his muscles might start to eventually function. "It's not an exact science," she says. "It's more like a crapshoot. It may work and it may not. In Mike's case I think it was fairly key to his recovery."

Mike's left side was quite a bit stronger than his right; he would jokingly refer to his weak leg as the tortoise and his strong one as the hare. As Maura puts it, their main goal was to "go after the tortoise," both with the use of FES and more traditional forms of therapy.

"When he first came in, he couldn't move that right leg because of the way his spinal cord had been damaged," she explains. "He couldn't straighten his knee, he couldn't move his ankle or bend his hip. In his arm, he couldn't bend his elbow completely.

"One of the things you need to do when you stimulate electrically is get your joints to bend," she says. "You've got to get all the muscles working together, otherwise, you can't advance your leg. It's a grind and very repetitive. But you have to look at the act of walking in segments. The micro stuff is very important.

"The nerve coming out of the spinal cord needs to communicate with a muscle or an action for a movement to happen," she adds. "That movement may be very weak at first. But it picks up over time in strength and endurance, and, after a while, you can stop using the electrical stimulation and just concentrate on the muscles and joints."

Simply put, the electrical stimulation helped Mike make the kinds of movements he could not make on his own. "In those early days, there was a lot of moving his leg through very heavy electrical stimulation," says Maura. "For instance, in his ankle, you could stimulate an upward movement. We did that for maybe a month for two hours a day, and then you started to see these little flickers of movement."

According to Whittaker, that tiny flicker of movement in Mike's ankle was a remarkably positive sign. "It meant that a message was going right down from the cord to the lowest part of the body," she explains. He was starting to get control of his foot by himself. We didn't need the electrical stimulation anymore, which meant we could start strengthening the muscles."

⚬⚬⚬

After the phase of electrical stimulation was complete, Maura and Mike began exercises that would strengthen the muscles required for standing. It's a phase she describes as repetitive and that requires a huge effort. "Some of the exercises were very painful," Mike admits. "It really hurt to stretch." But without the function of those muscles, he would simply collapse while attempting to remain upright.

In addition to stretching, Mike would undergo exercises on numerous machines that would act as facilitators for the activities he would eventually do on his own if all went well. For example, he would be strapped to a tilt machine, which would give him the sensation of standing and thus help his body know what it should be doing in the standing position. There was also the arduous task of learning how to use a transfer board, a tool that acted as a kind of bridge between someone lifting him out of bed and into his wheelchair, and being able to do so completely on his own. "You have to be able to transfer yourself without the board before you can really go forward," says Mike. "It's one of the most important steps."

Sometimes, the sessions lasted for up to two hours at a time. And Maura would frequently bring Mike back after a brief rest to do more strengthening exercises—often up to three times a day. "I feel that the more you can hit the nervous system, the better. We had nothing to lose and Mike's independence was really excellent."

෴

One of the crucial steps in the development of Mike's progress was getting his weak leg gradually used to the idea of resistance. At first, Maura put his leg in a sling and moved it around with the aid of pulleys. She did this to get his leg moving without the aid of gravity. During this "swing phase" she would gradually add a little more resistance to the process. As soon as this phase was mastered, the sling would be removed and Mike's leg could be manipulated through assisted movement. As his muscles began to improve, Maura would take away any support so that he could try lifting his leg on his own.

As Maura explains, a basic description of the process can't begin to capture the slow and grinding sense of repetition that is the product of going beyond each phase. "It's definitely incremental," she says, adding that a muscle isn't really functioning to useful capacity unless you can repeat an action ten or fifteen times. "After you see that strength, that's when you really start pushing for endurance."

There's a standardized assessment of muscle strength that determines when a patient like Mike is ready to go on to the next phase. "You don't want to set someone up for failure," says Maura. "You concentrate on an exercise that's going to be a success."

❧❧❧

On some days, Mike's progress was gauged by his sustaining a position or movement for mere seconds. "We had to give him a reclining chair because he couldn't even sit up," she recalls. "He was so debilitated by his injury that he could only lay on his back or his side. It hurt for him to lie on his stomach."

In fact, Maura relates that Mike's ability to turn over on his stomach marked a key turning point in the first stages of therapy. "I would hover around him nervously while he was on his stomach for about thirty seconds. Then we increased it to forty-five."

Once Mike could roll onto his stomach, the next step was getting him to sustain a crawling position on his hands and knees. When he could do this, he would have to learn to push himself up from a prone position.

"People think, it's just a matter of getting up and walking," says Whittaker. "But if you can't do all these other things along the way—like lie on your stomach or push yourself to your knees—walking is going to be impossible."

Mike had to learn to get up on his knees, even though sustaining this kind of upright position was extremely difficult for someone with his kind of injury. "It took an immense amount of effort to roll over and get up on my knees," he recalls. "I remember moments like that very clearly because they were so tough."

Maura recalls the first time Mike was able to sustain an upright position on his knees while on the mat. In evangelistic tones, he joked, "I feel a speech coming on."

～๑๑～

In addition to working on his lower body, Mike was undergoing occupational therapy to strengthen the use of his hand. As Rob explains, Mike's left hand was stronger than his right. "There was a diagonal thing happening with his body in terms of strength," he says. "Because the strength in his arms and hands were opposite to the strength in his legs."

113

"He had some basic hand movements," recalls Rob. "But he couldn't get a strong pinch. He couldn't grab and pull. Sensation was also a big issue because, while he had the motor control, there was a feeling of numbness and thickness in his fingers. So his eyes would have to give him the feedback that his sensation normally did."

Mike needed to learn to look at the things he wanted to pick up before he did so. However, that was only part of the story. "Once we determined that his hands were strong enough, we'd spend days and days doing the same basic tasks repeatedly," says Rob. "Mike would work on things like pinching and using a screwdriver. The repetition is valuable because it starts to reinforce communication between the brain and the hand until it becomes second nature again," explains Rob.

While such tasks were dull, Rob notes that Mike kept at them with an intense focus. In fact, his unusual diligence presented a unique problem. "Mike was so motivated that the most difficult challenge was slowing him down," Rob remembers. "Because the body is still recovering, you have to let it dictate the pace, otherwise you risk burning out. It took Mike a couple of weeks to realize that you can't just push all the time."

According to Rob, part of Mike's success in therapy was striking a balance between his own goals and the advice of his health-care team. "Mike is very goal-oriented and analytical," he says. "But he also listens, takes in the information, and thinks about it. He's a take-charge kind of guy, but he was never arrogant about it. He always made me feel that I had something valuable to offer."

It didn't take long for Mike to find his ideal pace, even though it was definitely slower than what he was used to before the accident. As he told the *Vancouver Sun's* Lori Culbert, his rehab style came from the hard-scrabble philosophy of former Green Bay Packer football coach Vince Lombardi. "You just pound out the yards and grind out the downs," he said, explaining that a day's therapy often resulted in gains that resembled "three yards and a pound of dust."

There were many things to relearn. Work at the bathroom sink—everything from using a toothbrush to learning how to hold and use his electric razor with a Velcro strap attached. Even something as second nature to Mike as putting on his glasses was now a chore, and yet his upper extremities were in better shape than his lower ones, so tasks such as putting on trousers proved even more difficult.

⌒⌒⌒

Mike's patience would begin to pay off with noticeable dividends. Learning how to write his name again was just one example. It also provided an example of a situation where Mike would learn to use the technique of visualization—simply shutting his eyes and imagining successfully accomplishing a task before trying to undertake it. (Visualization is taught at the rehabilitation centre, and is also taught in many other spheres of life.

Often part of meditation, the technique can be used to accomplish anything imaginable, from overcoming the fear of flying to changing one's entire life.)

In the case of learning to sign Mike's name, Rob and Mike started by using a pen encased in foam so it would be easier to hold. It took several weeks before Mike could attempt to write his signature within a three-line space. After much practice, he was able to use a regular ballpoint and sign his name in a single space.

For a confirmed list-maker like Mike, learning to use a pen again had special significance. "It's my old legal training," he explains. "I don't dictate. I've always written in longhand. Also, I tend to *think* through writing, so having the ability to pinch the thumb and forefinger together not only meant that I'd be able to write properly, legibly, and quickly. It also meant that I could organize my thoughts in a way that's comfortable."

Signing his name was just one of many tasks that Mike would learn to visualize in preparation for accomplishing the actual task. "As long as I knew where I wanted to go—and I could visualize it—then all of those painful incremental steps can be broken down into what I wanted to achieve within the next day or the next month," he says. "That was a real help. I'd just lie there as I was getting ready to go to sleep at night, close my eyes, and create a picture in my mind of where I wanted to be."

Sometimes Mike would visualize playing golf. In addition to walking out of G. F. Strong on February 28, another early goal that he had set involved playing golf with his buddies at a tournament in June. Given that he was still in a wheelchair—and unable to put on a golf shirt, never mind stand to swing a club—it may have seemed an unrealistic aspiration, but for Mike, this goal represented a vital part of the rehabilitation process.

"The doctors said they were doable," he recalls of his two most important objectives. "Getting there might be painful or onerous. But, for me, it was important to have those tasks as benchmarks."

And yet, there were days when the very idea of teeing off on a warm summer green must have seemed especially difficult to conjure up. While living at the rehabilitation centre, Mike would continue to be plagued by infections and high fevers. "My bowels were so unsteady that I couldn't go in the pool," he explains. "The part of therapy where you walk and swim in the pool was something I really missed, but I just couldn't do it."

C. difficile and the lack of control in his bowels would prove an ongoing difficulty throughout his time at G. F. Strong and beyond. "The bug was literally a pain in the ass," he says with a laugh. "It left me feeling messy and people were always cleaning up after me. There was nothing I could do about it, but that was really the most frustrating part of the whole process."

While Mike set daily and weekly goals, maintaining a positive outlook against the backdrop of such setbacks wasn't always easy. "I would have false starts and down times," he says. "I never doubted that I'd get out of G. F. Strong by the end of February, but there were times when I'd get frustrated."

❧

In January, Mike was able to attend his first public meeting on behalf of the Fraser Basin Council. One of British Columbia's most active and influential groups on issues of the environment and sustainability, the organization is close to Mike's heart. So much so that he gave a brief speech to more than 200 concerned environmentalists from his wheelchair. He received a prolonged standing ovation when Justen wheeled him out. The crowd's response moved him to tears. "That was a very emotional outing," he says. "Just because a lot of friends and people I knew were there. And I was able to be engaged again—to talk about something I really believed in."

Still, there were many other events Mike couldn't attend because of the ravages of infection. He found this frustrating. But whenever he felt the frustration of fighting the bug on top of mounting fatigue, he would try to focus on some of the lighter things at G. F. Strong.

❧

One of the things that gave Mike the most pleasure during his time at G. F. Strong was the bond he formed with other people on the second floor as a result of having organized a betting pool for the Vancouver Canucks' hockey games. A number of people on the floor—from nurses to patients—became involved in the pool. It gave them all an opportunity to focus on something other than the rigours of rehab. Everyone became closer because of the experience.

Mike got the idea from a rehabilitation counselor who'd organized a pool for Monday Night Football. When the counselor left at the end of football season, Mike decided to continue the tradition with hockey. "It was a fun sort of thing," he says. We'd order in pizza and bet on the games. There were a lot of young sports-oriented guys in the place and it helped to keep them motivated."

Mike's job was to "collect the dough." He chuckles, adding, "It was strictly volunteer and a lot of work, but I wasn't taking a cut or anything." As Beckie remembers, this event proved quite popular. At times, she would come in to read Mike poetry and discover him counting out bills. "Mike's bedside drawer was always full of money," she recalls with a laugh. For Mike, the hockey pool provided welcome relief from the stresses of rehab. He would also organize outings for his fellow patients, including attending a Vancouver Giants hockey game.

A friend who came to visit Mike at G. F. Strong noticed how much fun everybody was having while watching the Canucks games on TV. He struck up a conversation with a mother of one of the younger patients on the floor. "I mentioned that Mike seemed to be livening up the place quite a bit," he said. "The mother looked at me and said, 'This is the first time I've seen my son smile in months. And it's all because of that guy over there.' She was pointing at Mike."

Rob Giachino also noticed that Mike's spirit brought something special to the place. "Every once in a while we get clients coming through who really spice up the floor," he remarks. "There's just this increase in energy—this hum of activity when they're out and about. Mike was definitely one of those guys. He built up a lot of camaraderie that clients could relate to, regardless of age or injury level.

"Mike's got this larger than life personality," Rob adds. "But he's also very down to earth. He was open to playful jabs and he hung out with eighteen- and twenty-year-olds on a level that was equal. He knew all the clients' names, all the names of their relatives and everyone on staff. It was really nice."

For Rob, this demonstrated Mike's natural affinity for simply being one of the guys. "As goal-oriented as Mike is, he knows what he's lost and he knows how it's affected his family," says Rob. "He's always been in a position of control and this was very much the reverse, but he never let that get in the way. He was just great."

"I like people," Mike confides. "I've always been curious about their stories and who they are, even as a kid." He recalls a story his mother likes to tell. Mike was two years old and traveling by train with his mother. It was during the Second World War and the Harcourts were rendezvousing with Frank, who was serving in the navy. "I'd just wander around the train and walk up to somebody and say hi," explains Mike. He remembers encountering a brigadier general who was bringing a set of toy soldiers to his grandson. "My mother found us playing toy soldiers together on the floor," he says, laughing.

At the same time, Giachino feels that Mike's colleagues on the floor gave him back something special as well. "Rehab is a humbling process," he remarks. "I think if Mike had done therapy in isolation, he might have been a little more disappointed in things. But when you see everyone else on the floor, you quickly realize how lucky you are. That's why I think the effect of his time at G. F. Strong was very profound in both directions."

In fact, Mike would draw much-needed inspiration from the patients and staff on the second floor. It seemed as if every time he entered into a conversation with a fellow patient, he heard another story of hope and determination. Another example of people coping with profound change by moving forward against the odds. "All you had to do was listen to people and the message was clear," says Mike. "It was like, 'Hey, things aren't so tough for me. I can deal with it.'"

There was Helen Hadikin, a spirited woman in her seventies who had raised a daughter as a single mother and now found herself confined to a wheelchair. "She had just overcome cancer only to get this infection in her spine, which paralyzed her," recalls Mike. "But she was so upbeat and friendly, so determined to live on her own. We called her Saint Helen."

Mike also recalls a young man named Dave Culver who broke his back in a mountain-biking accident. "He was an instructor at the University College of the Cariboo teaching aspects of adventure tourism like whitewater kayaking," explains Mike. "The doctor told him he would never walk again, but he would painfully haul himself up in a back brace and crutches. That's how he learned to walk."

Mike felt especially touched by the story of his roommate, Bob Franken, a retired university professor suddenly afflicted with a rare spinal infection. "He was exhausted and the next morning he woke up paralyzed," says Mike. "It was a one in seven-million chance." Franken's specialty had been motivational psychology. And, while there were certain drawbacks to rooming together, Mike knew he had found a kindred spirit.

"We got along really well, even though he snored," Mike jokes. "You'd just get use to the rhythm of it and he'd change the snore pattern. So I'd kid him and he'd say, 'You snore too.' And I'd say, 'Good, I can get you back.'"

Mike would eventually get Franken to work with Rick Hansen, but in the meantime he and Franken found that their personal situations acquired deeper meaning by finding ways to address the common good.

"Bob and I made a list of ten things that needed to be changed at G. F. Strong," says Mike. "It was a whole range of things, from the fact that one of the elevators would close too quickly to accommodate wheelchairs to refining the goal-setting process. We gave them the list and they started to work on it."

Mike never let anything get in the way of his overall objectives. "There were a thousand little steps in moving forward," he recalls. "But they were starting to add up." Mike vividly remembers the milestone of pulling himself up from his wheelchair to stand at the standing bar. It was a point that nobody felt certain he would get too.

"That was amazing because we didn't know whether my muscles would be able to pull me," he says. "We didn't know whether my body would have the foundation in an integrated way to be able to stand, let alone walk. That's why it was such a big, big moment. I mean, for me, it was really huge."

Maura also remembers the first time that Mike stood up at the bars with support at the end of January. "He just stood up at the bars," she says. "I was amazed because a lot of people feel faint when they get up that first time. Being upright is very challenging for them because the blood doesn't get to the brain like it should, but Mike got up and he was fine."

"There's a lot of emotion around standing because it's a genuine turning point for any patient," she adds. "There was a feeling of relief at becoming an upright person again."

"The first time he stood, it was for about two minutes," recalls Rob, who says that Mike was strapped into a special device designed for the purpose that is known as a standing frame. "He was on his elbows really hard and his head was forward in posture a little bit. But he hadn't used his legs in months."

From there, they concentrated on getting Mike to sustain a low pivot—with his feet on the floor and while bent ove, a position that he needed to master in order to be able to get off the toilet and shower bench without help. Before too long Mike could stand longer and straighter, leaving one hand to stabilize himself and free the other hand for squeezing a ball or moving around blocks, an act, that as Rob explains, leads directly to such sink work as reaching for something from the medicine cabinet without losing your balance.

"Eventually Mike was able to stand for up to forty minutes, with one hand stabilizing him and the other just moving simple blocks around," says Rob. "We just started putting on those layers. While this was happening some of the sensation in his hands was returning."

The team also concentrated on getting Mike to walk with the aid of support. Mike worked at this with an intense focus, and Maura recalls that by mid-February he had moved from a walker to crutches. Watching him, she knew he would attain his goal of walking out of G. F. Strong by the end of the month.

Learning to walk again was almost like a new experience for Mike. As he points out, he had to keep many instructions in mind. "It was like there was always this tape playing in my head," he recalls. "Put your shoulders back. Put your heels so you can come down on the ball of your foot. Don't drag your foot." He laughs, adding that he could often hear an inner voice barking, "Heels! Heels! Heels!"

As Mike's gait improved, Maura would time his pace. "At one point, Maura said, 'If you're going to cross the street and make it in time with the walk sign on, you've got to get back to a metre a second,'" Mike remembers. "Finally, I was walking at a pace where I could get across a busy intersection while the walk sign is on and make it across like anybody else."

With much practice, the pace and speed of Mike's gait continued to show improvement. "I looked at him long and hard," says Maura. "I could see that he was safe on his feet—that he wasn't going to collapse. It wasn't a gamble, but it was a bit of a judgment call. The day he left, he hadn't been walking and out of his chair for even a week.

"Once you start walking, then you start to add function," she says. "Can you get up on your feet the first time rather than having to try three or four times? Can you climb stairs?"

Mike's ability to move around on crutches once he got home was crucial as far as Maura was concerned. "I have a thing about people going out in wheelchairs," she adds. "Because if they go out in a chair, they'll probably use the chair more than they should."

A long road of recuperation lay ahead, including Mike's difficult adjustment to a world that isn't always accessible to people on crutches. Still, as Maura states, everyone at G. F. Strong felt deeply proud that he achieved his goal of leaving the place by putting one foot ahead of the other.

"He was able to do what he set out to do," she says. "He fought very vigorously not to get derailed from his goals. His skill was being able to hone in on something, work like a dog for an hour, and be 110 percent there before switching to something else. Nothing could sway him, even though there were a lot of things vying for his attention."

For Whittaker, Mike's progress is just one example of why her work is so rewarding. Seeing patients return to a life where they can regain some of their independence and self-esteem is habit-forming.

"People ask me, 'How can you do this sort of work? It must be so depressing.' But it's actually quite the opposite," she explains. "The transformation that happens from day one is amazing. It may not add up to walking, but it adds up to basic function. They go from being totally dependent to learning how to live independent lives. There's a lot of satisfaction in that.

"Mike was grateful to everyone, from the people in the kitchen to the people who mop the floors and do the maintenance," she adds. "That's because the whole process is very personal. We're like a little family and he responded to that.

"We're stepping over things and managing on old equipment," she notes. "Sometimes the equipment is even homemade. It can be very chaotic, but it works because the dedication and the know-how is there, and it's hard to put a cost benefit analysis on that."

Rob Giachino feels that seeing Mike go through rehab on such a public level has a lasting effect. "On a kind of odd level, it helps for others to see a person like Mike go through his kind of injury," he observes. "It helps them realize that while there are certain physical changes, there are actually some things that don't change. Sort of like, 'This is who he *was* and we loved him then. Now, this is who he *is* and we still love him.'"

While the entire country was focused on whether Mike would walk out of G. F. Strong, there was an even more important message beyond his personal success as he walked out the door. "It just seems that he drew the spinal cord world and the normal world a little closer in terms of awareness," says Rob. "Now, he's involved with so many different levels in terms of accessibility, so it's a real bonus for all our future clients to have a Vancouver that's a little more accepting and a little more accessible."

In Mike's journey of a thousand steps, leaving G. F. Strong under his own steam seemed a major leap. With Justen by his side, Mike achieved his goal of walking out the door on crutches. It was a proud moment. But outside the sheltered environment of the hospital and the clinic, a whole new world awaited, a world that, in its own way, would prove every bit as uncompromising as any challenge Mike had ever faced.

6

THE LONG CLIMB BACK

"I'm not the type of person who tells Mike he can't do things. Besides, I know him very well. He eventually finds a way to get where he needs to go."
— BECKIE HARCOURT

A widely circulated newspaper photo shows Mike lifting his crutches off the ground as if they're wings, with his feet fully supporting him. The famous Harcourt grin seems so jubilant that it would be easy to overlook his unhealthy pallor. The picture ran as he was going home after months of institutionalized care. Although he was back on his feet, with the aid of crutches, a whole set of new challenges awaited him. Maura's advice was something Mike would try to keep in mind: Take things slowly, otherwise you'll risk a fall.

In fact, Mike's daily life would have to move at a more gradual pace once he returned home. "Learning to use walkers, crutches, and catheters is humbling," he explains. "Everything seems to take at least twice as long. There are so many new details to deal with that weren't a part of your daily life before. But what choice do you have? These are the things that allow you to get on with your life. It's all part of taking care of business."

⌇⌇⌇

"At the end of that first week, we saw how hard this was going to be," says Beckie. "I think what saved us was that we were able to talk about what was working and what wasn't. We spent a lot of time analyzing things and zeroing in on specific goals."

Goals ranged from meeting toilet and shower needs to holding utensils. "We'd really discuss the setbacks," she adds. "We set new goals for each week, which we reviewed at the end of the week. Then we had to focus on goals for the next week. What we were trying to do was make our life better little by little. We'd say, 'Let's just give this a try and then analyze it at the end of the week.'"

They would discover many things, both large and small. "It just seemed that we could see consistent improvements all the way along," says Beckie about why they decided to forgo nursing help. "Sometimes, they were tiny improvements. But we seemed to be moving in the right direction and that's what kept us going."

As exhausting as they found the process, the Harcourts also viewed it as deeply enriching. Ask Beckie what got her through the tough times and she replies, "It's all about unconditional love. You love your kid that way, especially when he's a baby. But it's not until you face something really extreme like this and work through it day by day that you realize certain things. This made me realize that Mike and I have an unconditional love."

For the Harcourts, Mike's trials strongly reinforced a lesson they had learned throughout their marriage. "We understood that we could solve various problems if we tackled them together," explains Beckie. "We'd change things and get results. It gave us strength and did a lot for our self-esteem."

Mike agrees. "Some people may think it's strange that you can gain so much insight from this kind of injury," he says. "But I really am learning more about myself. This kind of thing makes you so hugely grateful for family, friends, and the things that really matter. It was such an amazing feeling to get back to the environment that you love and the people you love."

As Beckie explains, they would both be energized by a circle of close friends, who would visit, call, or send encouraging notes. "Mike was always getting positive feedback about how well he was doing from people he really respected," she notes. "That kind of thing really makes a difference."

꿍ꍏꍏ

The world of an upright person recovering from a spinal injury is very different away from a controlled environment like G. F. Strong. It's not altogether unlike trying to negotiate a minefield of uneven sidewalks, slick floors, and high curbs with a set of two extra legs that you're still getting used to. Your body needs to take advantage of foreign equipment that's suddenly become a part of you. The adaptation process requires a great deal of patience.

Tight spaces were a problem. For a time, Mike would shower at his tennis club because it provided the wide stalls that could accommodate his walker. He was looking forward to helping Beckie with the evening meal, but there were still tasks that his hands couldn't manage. Unable to drive, he would have to rely on others to take him places. Even at home, he had to watch himself. Something as seemingly innocent as a throw rug had the potential to send him reeling.

Unfortunately, Mike was still doing battle with various infections, so, just when he needed the extra energy to cope with returning home, it simply wasn't there. "Mike had no immune system," explains Beckie. "So that was a problem. How do you put one foot in front of the other when you don't even have enough strength to get out of bed?"

"The first week I came home, I was a mess," Mike admits. "With the antibiotics and the drain on my energy, I had no control over my system. Beckie really saw what practical nurses see all the time. She'd have to clean me up and clean up the bathroom. One of my biggest worries was the stress that it was putting on Beckie."

"Quite honestly, Mike was having a ton of accidents," recalls Beckie. "I was doing endless loads of laundry and I was running around sterilizing every-thing. I was terrified that he was going to catch another infection."

Beckie remembers the first couple of months after Mike's return as one of the most stressful times of her life. "I'm a jogger," she says. "I mean, I *never* huff. But I was huffing and puffing all over the place. It was like running a marathon because I just had to keep going all the time."

Mike took comfort in the fact that Beckie has strength, intelligence, and tenacity, qualities that always seemed to come through when they were needed the most. "Beckie has tremendous talent," Mike remarks proudly. "If anything, she underplays it sometimes." One of Mike's favourite stories revolves around her teaching days when she was also doing graduate stud-ies in western Washington.

"She was in tears sometimes because she didn't think she would ever make it," says Mike. "But she ended up getting a 3.57 grade average, which really surprised her." However, Beckie's unassuming strength and courage never surprised Mike. It was a big part of what made them such a great team, a team unafraid to try new things to see how they might work out.

❧

Hiring a private nurse seemed an all-or-nothing sce-nario. Beckie and Mike would either need to commit to having someone move in around the clock or try to see if they could manage the situation themselves. They decided to put off getting a nurse until they could adequately measure the progress of Mike's recovery.

As Beckie explains, returning to a more private routine after months of dealing with so many different people had a definite appeal, despite the demands of Mike's home care. "We were grateful to have a life," she says. "Now we had to make it doable. We weren't really sure we could do it, but we wanted to start reclaiming a little bit of normalcy now that we were back in the house."

However, their desire to regain a certain degree of privacy would come with a price, including coping with the many changes in their domestic life. "During that first month or two, we weren't sleeping well," Beckie confides. "There was all the medical stuff and Mike's fevers. It was definitely a big adjustment."

"I notice the ebb and flow of my paralysis," says Mike. "It's a big issue. I get tired and it builds up. I can't sleep at night. But I'm dealing with the paralysis now rather than the question of Am I going to be in a wheelchair or not? It's a whole different set of circumstances. It's fabulous to know that I didn't have to use a transfer board and I wasn't going to have to go from a bed to a wheelchair or a wheelchair to a mat in a physio room."

Still, there were many tasks to carry out. While Mike would eventually learn to change his own catheter, the chore would initially fall to Beckie. "I'm not a nurse type," she admits. "When I was teaching, I could barely put a bandage on a kid, so I really didn't think that I could put a catheter in. That was something I never thought I'd have to learn."

On the other hand, more than thirty years of mutual trust gave Mike and Beckie the required skills for coping with all aspects of his rehab. "The tools are there so we can talk about the most intimate things," says Beckie. "Things we'd never talk about to anybody or ever thought we'd need to talk about."

The couple quickly developed a new routine that accommodated Mike's needs. Their regular bedtime was pushed ahead an hour so that Beckie and Mike could deal with Mike's toilet needs. Mike took regular naps, sometimes up to two hours a day. For a high-energy person like Mike, resting for long periods of time wasn't always easy. While his body felt exhausted, his mind would often be racing with thoughts of the many things he wanted to accomplish. But resting would have its advantages, including teaching him something about himself that he had been unaware of before the accident.

At VGH, Senator Jack Austin's wife, Natalie Freeman, had given Mike a book called *The Power of Now* by Eckhart Tolle. For someone who has spent his entire life moving toward new goals, the book contained valuable lessons. It taught Mike the benefits of simply focusing on the moment. "It made me realize that some of the chattering I was doing was about being addicted to talking," he says. "Reading the book made me understand that I had to work on listening to people without worrying about preparing an answer."

Mike laughs, adding, "That's a lot to learn for a list-maker like me. It's great to be focused and make things happen. But one of the things I learned from the accident is that there's a far broader reality. You can't be consumed by things. Sometimes, you just have to let go and surrender to the moment. I learned that there were times when I simply had to give in to my exhaustion."

Beckie explains that Mike's outlook proved a great help during those first weeks back home, especially since his adjustment to regular life had many setbacks. "We'd have a week where we felt we were really making progress and then we'd have a weekend where Mike had a fever and was flat on his back," she says. "So, at times, it was like taking three steps forward followed by one step back. It was such an intense time, and it didn't let up."

"I'd get frustrated a lot," Mike admits in regard to his low energy level. "But instead of exploding, I learned to rest. That would allow me to come back twice as determined."

⌒⌒⌒⌒

The three floors of the Harcourts' Vancouver residence weren't designed to accommodate someone with restricted movement. Off the main floor, there were many stairs leading down to the basement and also stairs that led up to the master bedroom on the third floor. Before Mike's accident, nobody gave much thought to the flights of stairs in their spacious, airy home. Now, each stair seemed to provide concrete evidence that Mike's recovery would continue to be a tough climb.

Like many other couples coping with a spinal injury, the Harcourts were compelled to re-evaluate the physical layout of their house. Mike would gain strength from thinking about the many people he had met at G. F. Strong who were determined to return to their own homes and make the required adjustments. "There were all sorts of stories about people who just wanted to make their lives work," he says. "Whether it's Bob Franken who had to pull all the carpeting out of his place to accommodate a wheelchair or a real estate agent who told me, 'If I can't go to an office anymore, I'll make an office in my home.'"

When a patient is about to move from G. F. Strong back to their regular environment, therapists will conduct a home study to gauge accessibility and consider the necessity of any possible structural modifications. Maura and Rob each did a home study with Mike and Beckie. When Rob made his first evaluation of the Harcourts' house before Mike's departure from G. F. Strong, Mike was still using the wheelchair and his prognosis was uncertain.

At first, Rob thought they might need to do major renovations to accommodate the use of a chair. "You have to make sure the house and the equipment are ready," Rob notes. "But you also have to make sure that the family is psychologically ready as well. Initially, we weren't sure how soon Mike was going to be able to use the stairs."

Mike, on the other hand, considered the stairs just another obstacle that he was eager to conquer. "I'm not an egomaniac," says Mike. "But I do have a strong ego. You need to have a pretty strong ego to think you can stop a freeway or initiate a whole different way of looking at cities." It also turned out to be a good attribute to possess when it came to conquering the stairs.

Beckie recalls that they discussed the option of creating a makeshift bedroom on the main floor. However, now that Mike was home, he felt determined to return to as much of his old routine as possible, and that meant climbing the stairs to the bedroom, however long it took. "I always have a really clear idea of what I want to see happen at any given time," he says. "There was nothing squishy or wishy-washy about it. I'm a jovial, pleasant sort of a guy, but I also have an iron will when it comes to achieving the checklist of things I want to accomplish."

As always, Mike relied on his lifelong ability to eliminate any outside distraction and concentrate on the task at hand. "It's like a basketball player who has to get the winning foul shot in the opposing team's gym," he remarks. "The fans are screaming and shouting, trying to psyche you out, but you focus on the image of the front rim and the ball floating through the hoop. You just screen everything else out."

Beckie vividly recalls when Mike walked up the stairs during that first home study with Rob. "I couldn't believe it," she says. It was in early February and he was still spending most of his time in the wheelchair. It was only at the end of February that he was on crutches."

As Beckie explains, "For other people, extreme stubbornness could be a really negative characteristic. But, in Mike, it's part of the reason why he's successful. I think it's because his strong will is combined with an equally strong sense of optimism. That combination has always been a very deep underlying strength."

As Mike's rehabilitation progressed at G. F. Strong, it became clear that major changes to the house wouldn't be necessary. Justen, who was preparing to begin graduate studies shortly, built a wheelchair ramp at the back of the house with a friend's help. Mike never used it. As Rob recalls, the initial list of home equipment kept getting pared down. "I think he ended up purchasing a cane and a shower bench," says Rob. "Just the basics."

✿

Although Mike's steady progress would ultimately allow him to dispense with a wheelchair, the household stairs would remain a concern. By the time Maura went through the house to check for accessibility, Mike was an outpatient at G. F. Strong and still in the early stages of getting used to walking with the support of a walker or crutches. He was also continuing to cope with *C. difficile*, which—after a welcome respite—had "returned with a vengeance" at the end of January.

While doctors prescribed a last-resort remedy, which Mike refers to as "the mega-bomb of antibiotics," the medication had yet to kick in during his first week at home. "Exhaustion was a problem," recalls Mike. "I was really low on both physical and psychic energy." All of which made the ability to repeatedly go up and down the stairs a daunting proposition.

"To be quite honest, I kind of gasped when I saw all those stairs," says Maura, of her first look at the Harcourt home. "Stairs take a lot of strength and they can be a real barrier to mobility, so this was a very big deal."

Maura remembers Mike telling her that he intended to work on climbing the stairs while carrying the paper and two cups of coffee up to Beckie. A morning ritual that Mike had performed for many years prior to his accident, it was always a special way for the couple to start their day. Now, it meant that Mike would have to go up the stairs without using a free hand to steady himself on a railing. "I didn't encourage that," says Maura with a laugh. "I thought, My God, if you can just get your body up those stairs, you'll be doing fine."

With Mike's weakness from the infection, a precarious sense of balance, and the remaining numbness in his hands, carrying coffee up the stairs took a while to work out. When someone suggested that he could carry one cup of coffee up the stairs at a time, Mike laughed. "There was no way I was going to make two trips," he says.

At first, Mike tucked the paper under his arm and carried a cup of coffee in each hand. The method proved slow and awkward. "I didn't tumble," he recalls. "But the coffee mug would slip in my hand and I'd get coffee on the carpet."

However, coffee stains on the carpet seemed a small price to pay for Mike's efforts. Beckie understood that she had to let her husband keep plugging away until he got it right. "I knew that Mike was trying to rebuild a part of our life," she explains. "It may seem like a small thing, but it was a pleasant part of our day that we always enjoyed." She laughs, adding, "I'm not the type of person who tells him he can't do things. Besides, I know him very well. He eventually finds a way to get where he needs to go."

✂≈✂

With all the changes Mike had undergone since the accident, Beckie found it comforting that so many things about her husband's character remained constant. His diligence had a plus side. It showed he was still a *doer*. This proved especially true when it came to Mike's passion for problem solving.

"Even though he was very weak, he still seemed like the old Michael," she says. "Bringing me coffee was something he could focus on. For me, it meant he was dealing with things. Some of his goals may have been different since the accident, but he was still focusing in on them."

"I sometimes half-jokingly describe myself as a competitive co-operator," says Mike. "I'm into co-operation, but I'm also highly competitive. I like to win." For Mike, winning meant setting the bar as high as possible. Even for something as straightforward as bringing up a cup of coffee.

Eventually, at Beckie's suggestion, Mike began to use a tray to balance the paper and both cups of coffee. "If you're going to bring up coffee, it has to be on a tray," she says with a smile. "Of course, that ups the ante and makes it even more difficult." It was yet another illustration of how much Beckie understood the factors that have always motivated her husband.

"The tray was a huge challenge," recalls Mike, who notes he was still spilling coffee on the carpet. But, with patience and practice, he was eventually able to bring the coffee up the stairs without spilling a drop. He remembers the moment as a clear victory for preserving a part of his old life while getting on with his new one.

For Mike, getting back to the daily rituals of his former life was important, even if he couldn't perform them with the same degree of speed or efficiency. One thing that helped get him though the rough spots was his attitude toward his diminished physical capabilities. His strong sense of competition aside, he was developing a new way of measuring progress. It wasn't just how well he carried out a familiar task. He also found himself taking new pleasure in the simple joy of being able to perform that task at all.

"You know things are never going to be the same," he says, of Plan B. "But that's not the point. The point is to enjoy the things you used to do to the best of your ability, to take nothing for granted. That's what's really important."

Beckie agrees: "Every day there was some new thing to achieve and be grateful for Mike, and I learned to celebrate every one of those moments."

~☙~

By March, there were any number of moments to celebrate. For one thing, Mike's health was steadily improving. He had managed to avoid a major infection for weeks and the antibiotics combating *C. difficile* had finally kicked in to help stabilize his toilet habits. He was also beginning to spend more time on a major part of Plan B—becoming re-engaged in his passion for aboriginal issues and sustainable cities.

That month a beaming Mike would stand beside Justen as Beckie received a medal for bravery from the Commonwealth Awards for Honour and Rescue. Beckie would tell the media, "It's what anybody would have done. I am very honoured and very grateful." For Mike, seeing the love of his life being publicly acknowledged for her courage was one of his proudest moments ever. Looking at pictures of the event, it hardly seemed possible that Mike had been clinging to life only months before.

Gradually, Mike would begin to get out for trips around the neighbourhood. As always, he set daily goals. A half-hour walk around the neighbourhood for fresh air. A stroll to his neighbourhood barber. He even managed to attend a packed Bruce Springsteen concert, an event that was especially meaningful since Mike had used Springsteen's music to get pumped up for rehab.

The more he went out, the more Mike understood the effect his injury had on others. "I get between ten and fifteen people a day stopping me to say how much I've inspired them," he says. "It was startling at first, but then I realized that what's happened to me has a powerful and lasting impact on people who find them-selves going through any tough situation."

"A lot of people have health issues," adds Beckie. "And they knew that Mike had to start from scratch in terms of learning how to walk. Other people thought, if Mike can do this, then I can deal with my illness. Or I can relearn what I need to do because of my stroke."

✦✦✦

Like just about everything else in Mike's life, his im-proving health was the product of much thought. His health regime relied on the wisdom of bringing in the best team possible. In addition to his doctors at G. F. Strong, Mike wanted to draw on the wisdom of Vancouver doctors Hal Brown and Larry Chan, who specialized in naturopathic and holistic medicine. Shortly after leaving the rehabilitation centre, he began to address his health problems by integrating a holistic approach.

Before his accident, Mike had been their patient for about twenty years. His positive experiences with acupuncture and the ancient Chinese practice of chi-gong convinced Mike that these two specialists would play a positive role in his rehab. "I was determined to use alternative approaches to supplement more conventional treatments," says Mike. "I didn't want to be limited to traditional medicine."

A number of potential treatments were considered for Mike's integrated recovery program, everything from traditional medical doctrine to such radical treatments as oxygen chamber therapy, which both Dr. Townsend and Dr. Chan ultimately struck from Mike's program. Mike recalls the discussion between the rehab doctor and the naturopath with the abiding fascination of someone who has always believed in the power of co-operation. "This discussion they had was really quite extraordinary," he says. "It was an hour long—a very respectful dialogue between two hugely talented professionals who expressed their own viewpoint while reaching across those disciplines extraordinarily well."

The dialogue was especially important to Mike since he attributes one of the reasons for his excellent health to a strong interest in alternative medicine, an interest he pursued prior to his injury. Dr. Hal Brown agrees. "Mike was very keen on optimizing his health," says Dr. Brown of Mike's health regimen prior to the accident. "He was starting to eat better, he started to exercise better, and he lost some weight. He was actually in very good shape. It was a good testament to natural health care."

Before his accident, Mike had sought naturopathic treatment for shoulder and back problems. "In terms of strength and energy I think he was probably doing better than most people his age," Dr. Brown notes. "He was golfing, skiing, and playing tennis. We were just optimizing his well-being with various tools."

After the accident, Dr. Chan and Dr. Brown worked out a specific program to deal with Mike's injury. "Larry did the holistic medical approach," says Mike. "A whole series of things like the DSO sulphide treatment [a series of injections to aid in the restoration of the nerve cells] that got me ready for Hal's acupuncture."

"We just sort of carried on in a more intense way," explains Dr. Brown. "Mike was having problems with his bowels and his bladder so we did what we could to provide some support in that area. We were also looking at what we could do to help promote some sort of therapeutic activity at the spinal cord injury level.

"Obviously, that's a very challenging area," says Dr. Brown of taking a naturopathic approach to Mike's spinal injury. "We don't have a lot of research in that area, so we relied on some things that we knew and we did some of our own research. We came up with a program supporting the spinal cord, using a lot of antitoxins, fatty acids, and Chinese herbs."

He explains that the first order of business was to address Mike's discomfort: "We put him through a course of ozone therapy to oxygenate the body as much as possible. You want oxygen to heal the spinal cord." This course of therapy was done through an IV drip.

Part of Mike's treatment included acupuncture, which involves the application of needles at strategic points in the body. "In Chinese medicine, the theory is that there's a flow of energy in the body," explains Dr. Brown. "We call it the *chi* energy, which is basically life force energy. In acupuncture, there are lines that flow up and down the body and the energy flows along those lines, and that's been measured electromagnetically. We know that it happens.

"So the basic concept is that when we do acupuncture, we're trying to manipulate that energy, to move it towards areas of injury to promote healing."

In addition to acupuncture, Mike also continued the practice of chi-gong—a physical and mental exercise that moves the body's energy to promote healing. Combined with some other naturopathic treatments Mike was undergoing—along with more traditional aspects of his health-care regime—he began to see results.

"I could feel the flow of the *chi* like a sort of flush," he says. "I felt like I was building up my reserves of strength with the naturopath—with vitamins and fish oil. I didn't mind being a kind of guinea pig if the treatment could also be used by other people."

Dr. Brown feels that Mike's understanding and acceptance of alternative treatments definitely helped the healing process. "I think if we just did acupuncture on somebody who wasn't particularly interested and was a little more cynical, it would just be somebody sticking needles in you," he says. "But Mike understood the experience through his practice of chi-gong. He was working on moving that energy himself, and he very clearly experienced the enhancement of that energy flow. That's why his perspective was so valuable in his support of treatment."

⌒⌒⌒

Dr. Brown likens Mike's recovery to a number of elements coming together in perfect harmony, including the different aspects of his health care. "To me, it's like a symphonic experience," he explains. "You don't go to a symphony and hear the bass first and then the horns. It doesn't work that way. The magic happens when everything blends together. I think Mike is a good example of someone who had all the elements of the orchestra working for him."

One of the key elements was Mike's attitude. Dr. Brown recalls the sense of optimism Mike brought to his treatment, despite the many challenges that resulted from his injury. "Mike is one of the most upbeat guys I know," he observes. "Having said that, I'd like to point out that you can be a happy well-adjusted person and still suffer greatly, and Mike clearly suffered. He went through hell."

All of which made his appetite for life even more impressive. "You can put Mike in a room with anybody and within fifteen minutes he'll know their life story," says Dr. Brown, who adds that he's learned a lot from Mike's attitude toward the accident. "Sometimes, I'd think, who's getting the treatment here?" he observes.

"Nobody ever considers how much a doctor can get from a patient, but I learned a lot from Mike."

For Mike, his attitude is nothing special. It simply reflects a desire to maintain a passion for the many things he enjoys, whether it's finding out more about a person as they sit in a doctor's waiting room or getting back to life on Pender Island.

Dr. Don Williams recalls the first time he saw Mike on the island again after the accident. "The thing that amazed me was how quickly I encountered him on Pender Island long before I expected to," he says. "It was in the early spring and he was standing on crutches talking to all these people around him. The sun was shining and he was smiling. It was just wonderful to see him."

⊱⊰

Typically, Mike would joke to his fellow islanders that he now had the strongest patio railing around. But, on a deeper level, he took the support of friends very seriously. This included the idea of playing golf with his buddies in June, a goal that had been moving closer since his last days at G. F. Strong when he would practise hitting a plastic whiffle ball out on the grass.

In order to reach that goal, he needed to achieve several other goals by June, including everything from getting off the catheter to weaning himself off crutches and then a cane. "The tournament would show that I was becoming more independent, more mobile, and less reliant on other people having to do stuff for me," he says. "It meant that I could walk up and down the hazards and the rolling hills. It also meant that I could travel because I'd be able to get in and out of cars and hotels, so it was like literally getting back into the swing of things."

Apart from all that, the tournament was important because it provided a fun way for Mike to enjoy several long-standing friendships. "The guys and I have been playing golf together for about eight years," he says. "But I've known some of them since high school. We kid each other a lot."

By the time Mike made it to the golf tournament, he was down to the occasional use of a cane for longer distances. Of course, things had changed considerably since the last time he had played a few holes. Still, as far as his golfing buddies were concerned, all the important things remained the same. "They were glad to see me, but they gave me the usual hard time and vice versa," says Mike. He laughs, adding, "We know each other so well that we could blackmail each other, but we don't."

The changes Mike noticed in his golf game seemed unimportant. "I wasn't a long ball hitter, but I hit it even shorter after my accident," he says. "I half jokingly said, 'I'm now playing like an eighty-five-year-old Scotsman, and I can still beat you guys.' It was great to get back to that kind of thing, plus I discovered that I actually putt better with the paralysis because it doesn't allow you to over-putt."

Better yet, it would often seem as if one goal naturally led to the next. For example, Mike's ability to drive a golf cart that June led to him driving a car again in August. The doctors left it up to Mike to decide when he wanted to get behind the steering wheel again, so, once he mastered the golf cart, he began to get back into driving.

"I drove around the block and my reaction times were good," he recalls. "So I drove a little more. Finally, I drove out to visit my parents and it was fine."

Around that time, Beckie remembers bumping into the psychologist, who told Mike that he had to slow down. "She couldn't believe that he was actually driving a car," smiles Beckie. "But I knew as soon as he was driving a golf cart that it wouldn't be long. That's Mike."

Not that Beckie didn't have any concerns about his rapid progress. She recalls a trip to Ottawa Mike took at the beginning of June to attend a conference. A month before his scheduled flight, she didn't think he was ready to travel on an extended flight by himself. "I wasn't going to tell him that he couldn't go," she says. "But I was worried. The whole thing seemed so monumental because he was working so hard already."

However, for Mike, it was simply a matter of breaking down the individual tasks until they were doable. He practised everything over and over. Tying his shoes, buttoning his collar, picking up his pace until he knew he could make it through an airport. Shortly before the flight, Beckie noticed a change in Mike. "Something just came together," she says. "It was like he reached down and pulled something deep out of his reserve."

Beckie remembers dropping Mike off at the airport. It was only after he had boarded the plane that she realized something seemed different. "Mike had forgotten his cane in the car," she says. "He just walked away without it." Later Mike would joke with his friend Vicki Gabereau that he kept leaving his cane behind without thinking to pick it up. "I figured it was trying to tell me something," he explained. "Like 'Goodbye.'" But this was a first. For Beckie, driving back home with Mike's walking stick still in the car meant one thing: Mike was ready to fly in more ways than one.

7

THE ACCESSIBLE CITY: BREAKING DOWN DISABILITY BARRIERS

"Mike's journey is representative of the journey that everybody is on. We all have goals and dreams, and stuff happens to us, but it's how you deal with it that makes the difference."
— RICK HANSEN

Rick Hansen recalls first meeting Mike Harcourt at a Vancouver city council meeting while trying to raise funds for his Man in Motion World Tour. Mike was mayor and Hansen, a 27-year-old young man with the dream of wheeling his chair around the globe to raise money for spinal cord research. It was the early 1980s, but the seventies' mindset about the disabled not getting their hopes too high still prevailed.

"It was such an ambitious and crazy goal," says Rick of the Man in Motion idea. "We were looking anywhere we could for funding, so we decided to try and get support from my home city. Mike graciously arranged for the opportunity to make a presentation to city council and ask for support."

"The council was polarized in their opinions," recalls Rick. "So we didn't receive any financial support." What Rick remembers most from that day is Mike's personal disappointment at the council's mixed reaction to the Man in Motion proposal. "Mike told us that we were doing a great thing and he wanted to wish us well," he says. "In fact, Mike felt so badly about the council's response that he reached into his pocket and gave us a personal donation on our way out the door. It was actually pretty funny and we laugh about it today, but it also says a lot about Mike's high level of awareness. He may have been a politician, but he always came across as a person first."

Mike recalls that particular council meeting as one of the few times he felt genuinely annoyed at some of his colleagues. "There were a few people on council who were being real jerks," he admits. "I just found what Rick had to say so inspiring. I couldn't believe that this guy was sitting in front of us talking about going around the world in a wheelchair."

༺☙☙༻

By mid-2004, after many months of rehab—and a diligent home workout and health program—Mike estimated that he had recovered about 80 percent of his capacity before the accident. And yet, with all the progress that he was making, he still had two major challenges to face. The first involved maintaining his 80 percent level of recovery through constant exercise and workouts at the gym. The second was seeing how much of the remaining 20 percent of his pre-accident capacity he could recover.

As Mike's doctor's told him, he might have leveled off at an 80 percent recovery. Nevertheless, he continued to set daily goals—tasks that could range from lifting weights at the gym to taking longer walks. "I don't know how much of my full capacity I'll get back," he says. "I may still have the same paralysis I have now—in my quads [the large muscles at the front of the thighs], my lower spine and gut, and in my hands. I hope I get some of that stuff back, but who knows if it will happen and how it will happen? You just have to keep working at it."

Mike had the same positive attitude about reactivating his commitment to social issues, especially those issues pertaining to spinal cord injuries. Now that the major part of his rehab process was finished he wanted to fulfill his promise to Marcel Dvorak, Rick Hansen, and the dozens of people he had met on the road to recovery. As he told Dr. Dvorak immediately after his operation, "As long as this has happened to me, why not use it to do good things?"

It's a philosophy that Rick Hansen understands better than most others. "As difficult and challenging as this has been for Mike, he will add incredible value to creating an awareness of the issues surrounding spinal cord injury," says Rick. "Not because of the awareness but because, from a personal perspective, he's connected to this and he wants to make a difference." Rick pauses, before adding, "And whenever Mike wants to make a difference, he usually does."

Rick recalls realizing when he visited Mike at G. F. Strong how his outlook could be a potent force for change. "He was holding court. He's got the whole team there, everyone from nurses to spinal cord patients." Remembering how encouraging Mike was to his fellow patients, he adds, "Mike probably gave more to others than he ever received."

While both Mike and the work he does on behalf of the disabled have a connection to public service, Rick believes that they ultimately transcend the traditional image of politics. "I think seeing him go through trauma and do it with such grace had a definite effect on people," says Rick. "And then to take that experience and use it to help others places him in a different category. A giving person with a face, a heart, and a soul—someone who has struggled and emerged through that struggle with great dignity along the way. That's why the outpouring of concern and sympathy has always been there."

For Rick, it simply re-enforces a lesson he learned through his own injury. "Mike's journey is representative of the journey that everybody is on," he says. "We all have goals and dreams, and stuff happens to us, but it's how you deal with it that makes the difference."

⋘⋙

One of Mike's proudest moments as mayor was seeing Rick off on his Man in Motion World Tour in 1985. The crowd was not especially large. However, two years later, when Rick returned to Vancouver having achieved his goal of wheeling around the world, throngs of people greeted him. To date, Hansen has raised more than one hundred and fifty million dollars for spinal cord research. But he's never forgotten that part of that money came straight out of Mike Harcourt's pocket at a time when he really needed it.

"You never know when you begin a relationship what common elements you'll share as you go through your life," says Rick. "People change and evolve and things happen, but Mike has always been committed to disability issues, both before and after his accident."

His injury aside, Mike's belief in providing full social resources to the disabled community has remained the same since he first became a community activist. "Every citizen should have a high quality of life," he affirms. "Disabled people shouldn't be stereotyped or have barriers in their way unnecessarily. It's enough of a barrier having a disability in the first place. At the very least, society should deal effectively with the unnecessary barriers that we can do something about."

⌘

Mike's latest role in the disability fight is an extension of the foundation he created during his political career. Mike first became active in disability issues as an experienced member of Vancouver's city council back in the 1970s. Like most major cities of that era, Vancouver was far from disability-friendly, a condition that Mike and other council members worked hard to change.

"I was very supportive of a lot of the changes put forward," says Mike. "Things like changing the building code to make public buildings more accessible. The disability committee kept coming up with new ideas. These little innovations that we introduced as we went along, like audible signals that the deaf could hear at crosswalks, just seemed to make a lot of sense, so we made those things happen."

When Mike became mayor, he was determined to push for more accessibility, putting funds into the lowering of city curbs to make it easier for people using crutches and wheelchairs to negotiate city streets. He also made some groundbreaking changes in the area of transportation for the disabled.

Revamping the Lions Club vans that were used to transport disabled kids, he initiated a modern program for the entire disabled community known as Handi-Dart. As part of Expo 86, Mike was also instrumental in awarding licences to a new taxi company whose cabs were specifically designed to serve people in wheelchairs.

Looking back on life after the accident, there's a certain serendipity for both Mike and Beckie in Mike's long service to the disabled. "These were issues that Mike worked on for decades as alderman, mayor, and premier," says Beckie. "As it turned out, Mike approved the disabled taxi that both he and his dad ended up using." As Mike puts it, "It never occurred to me that I'd actually be using the facilities I helped put into action. But, over the years, people in the disabled community kept presenting me with so many inspiring ideas."

One of those ideas was a pioneering condo development called Creekview. "We added six self-contained units that were available for people with spinal injuries," recalls Mike, who cast the deciding ballot as mayor in a very close vote.

Mike credits the idea for the development to disability activists Norm Haw and Walt Lawrence. Injured in a hockey accident as a young man, Walt was living at Vancouver's Pearson Hospital, a home for the seriously disabled that was straight out of the dark ages in more ways than one. Lawrence appeared before council in an electric wheelchair. Using a puff straw, he pleaded his case for a decent living environment with a conviction that touched Mike deeply.

"Walt was a hero," says Mike. "He literally broke out of Pearson. He liberated himself, saying he refused to stay in an iron lung or ventilator there because the people were too paternalistic. He wanted me to approve the Creekview Co-op, and I did."

Decades later, Walt Lawrence is married to a nurse, has two kids, and lives in the suburbs of Vancouver. "He's a counsellor at G. F. Strong who helps others deal with their injury," explains Mike, who would often see Walt during his time at the rehabilitation centre. "But it all started with Creekview."

∽⌒∾

Mike's interest in disability issues would carry over into his time in the premier's office, with the advisory committee on disabilities. "There was a whole series of things that needed to be done to expand the definition of disabilities," he recalls. "Quality of life also includes the attitude that others have towards people with disabilities," adds Mike. "Are they respected and understood? How often do you see someone leaning down and yelling at somebody who's in a wheelchair. You know something? They can hear you fine."

Mike's attention to disability issues was to become an integral part of his post-political career through his work with so-called sustainable cities, where the quality of life is improved without burdening future generations. As Mike points out, there are five major elements to consider when deciding how to make a city more accessible for the disabled: housing, transportation, employment, services, and quality of life.

"Sixty-two percent of people with spinal cord injuries are unemployed," says Mike, adding that the average is similar in a wide range of other disability communities. "So training after you're disability is important," he says, "We need to find a new and creative ways to take advantage of people's skills."

For Mike this means not only providing retraining in new occupations, but discovering ways that the victim of a spinal cord injury can find related work in a field they're already familiar with. "If you're a plumber with a spinal cord injury, what do you do?" he asks. "You can't crawl under buildings or sinks anymore, but maybe you can run a service for other plumbers where you do their accounts or order their supplies.

"Having access to services is crucial," explains Mike. "This is particularly true in small towns. There has to be a whole range of services, including physiotherapy services. But a high quality of life also includes being socially and culturally accepted as well. That means you have to consider such things as housing, transportation, and recreation. It's all part of what really makes an accessible city."

Without an effort to make these changes, an already difficult transition will prove even more challenging. "The adjustment isn't easy," notes Mike of life after a spinal injury. "It's a huge learning curve for everybody with a lot of pain along the way, not just for the person with the injury but for family and friends as well. It's catastrophic. You can't sugar-coat it and say, 'Gee whiz. Just be positive.' You have to make it doable."

Catching himself sounding especially passionate, Mike grins. "It's like that famous joke about the chicken and the pig each bringing something to the communal breakfast," he explains. "The chicken contributes by providing the eggs, but the pig is fully committed when he supplies the bacon. Before I was a chicken bringing the eggs. Now, in terms of disability issues, I'm much more like the pig. I have to live with partial paralysis every day. And that can't help but deepen my commitment."

ᄼᅩᄾᄼᅩ

His injury has also left him with memories and relationships that have deepened his commitment to disability issues in another way. He carries those memories with him every day. "It will always make a difference that I was right in the middle of people who were undergoing terrible tragedies," he says. "I could see the pain and I could hear it. Why make the adjustment tougher by leaving up barriers that are going to make it impossible to get around?

"It's something that you can't help taking with you into the disabled community when you start dealing with these broader issues," Mike continues. "As an experience, it's a great motivator to help make things better."

The reality of his injury also makes him more conscious of accessibility issues than ever before. Mike had first-hand experience with a large, inaccessible city when he went to visit Justen, who was settling into his studies at the London School of Economics. One thing he discovered was a lack of elevators and escalators.

"There were long corridors and long flights of stairs in the subway system with no elevators," he recalls. "If I had been in a wheelchair or on crutches, I would have been in a lot of trouble. The place I was staying in had four floors with no elevator and I was on the fourth floor.

"The problem is they're old buildings and an old subway system," explains Mike. "They're investing in making the tube system accessible with elevators. But retro-fitting it afterwards is a very expensive proposition. The problem of access is compounded when you realize how widespread the disability community is. Dealing with people who have spinal cord injuries is only one track," explains Mike. "The other track is the whole disability community. There are so many ties between the two tracks. They all face the same barriers."

Rick Hansen agrees. "While we hope that a new generation of people will have a better chance to walk away from their injuries, we still care about people living with spinal cord injuries, he says. "We have to do whatever we can to remove obstacles to a better life.

"Some of the greatest barriers are still out there," he cautions. "Problems with access to transportation, housing, jobs, or recreation. The more we can focus on accommodating communities that are aware and philosophically aligned, the more we can accelerate the standard for change. Mike's work in the community is all part of that, symbolically and personally."

Today, Mike is honourary chair of the Vancouver chapter of Rick Hansen's Wheels in Motion annual fundraising event. He also chairs the advisory committee on the development of the International Collaboration on Repair Discoveries Centre, commonly known as ICORD. This spinal-cord-injury research and therapy centre will be built on the site of the Vancouver General Hospital, and Mike hopes it will become the best such facility in the world. His specific area of interest is in how to make cities more accessible for the disabled.

"I've had a long friendship with Rick," says Mike. "It started out as a policy acquaintance relationship, but has deepened now that I have an emotional tie to disability issues. When I was mayor and premier, it just seemed like the right thing to do. Now being a partial quad makes it real in a whole other way. I'm right in the middle of it now and it's profoundly personal, so it's especially important to work with him on issues such as Wheels in Motion and ICORD.

"I feel lucky," he says. "Lucky to have had the support of family and friends throughout the process of rehab. But what about those people who don't have that kind of a support network? What about the ones who aren't so lucky? The only answer for them is that we have to *make* one. We have to ensure that there are certain things in place that future generations will be able to count on."

As Greg Latham, vice president of Rick Hansen's Man in Motion Foundation, explains, Mike's public service experience combined with the insight provided by injury makes him uniquely qualified for both his Wheels in Motion and ICORD positions. "He's got his finger on the pulse of the needs of researchers and their priorities," says Latham, who has more than thirty years' experience as a disability activist. "Not only is he a leader, but he's a leader who has been through all the stages of a spinal cord injury. He feels comfortable sharing what that's like with others.

"I just found him to be interested, open, and very giving," says Latham. "I can remember there was a lot of debate over whether Mike should be asked to help. And I got the job of asking him. His response was so amazing. There wasn't a fraction of a second of hesitation."

Latham feels that Mike's willingness to share so many of his own challenges through such vehicles as the series in the *Vancouver Sun* and Rick Hansen's Wheels in Motion Campaign, have had a positive effect on people's attitudes, an effect that will continue as long as Mike chooses to speak out. Latham observes that Mike's willingness to expose his own experience with rehabilitation can't help but remove some of the mystery from the process.

"I think people have fears about the possibility of something like this happening to them," says Latham. "If it could happen to Mike, it could happen to anybody. But talking about the people he met—the patients and the caretakers who were helping him through the process—was a real benefit. People could see that something good was happening along the way and it gave them hope.

"I've been watching Mike along the way," he continues. "Just seeing his progress is inspiring because it takes a lot of hard work to maintain his level of function. I see that determination as important, and I think others do as well."

However, as Latham explains, Mike's value to disability issues reaches far beyond the inspirational. His expertise on sustainable cities will be put to practical use both in terms of Wheels in Motion and ICORD.

He's aware that part of opening doors for the disabled means making sure they can literally get through the door as well.

"Mike really believes that we can eventually make the world a place where the only time you see a wheelchair is [in] a museum," says Latham. "But until that day, we need to focus on access. Participation in communities is greatly enhanced by simple things like barriers being removed in city halls, community centres, and places of work. This should be the case right across Canada."

While much work remains to be done, Mike believes many improvements have occurred. "If you look at each successive generation, things keep improving," Mike observes, of issues related to the spinal cord world. "The difference in techniques of surgery, the rehab techniques, and other opportunities are here because of the work of people like Rick and other pioneers. There's a big difference between having trouble with access to ramps because they're too steep and having no ramps at all."

༺༻

Rick explains that Mike's way of coping with his injury shows how a person can help others by helping himself. "The pain that people go through in terms of dealing with their accident is quite varied," he notes. "Some people never adjust to their circumstances. They always remain fixated on the pain, the suffering, and the disability.

"Other people—given time to go through a grieving process—inevitably reconcile where they're at. They start looking forward. Still others seem to be able to turn the page very quickly. I've met a few people like that and Mike is certainly one of them." Rick feels that Mike's recovery is the best example of someone who naturally combines his personal determination with a willingness to share his good fortune. "I see Mike as a representation of spinal cord injury that's not just a benevolent recipient of social goodwill," says Rick. "It's a cause that features a group of people who are ready, willing, and able to give something back to the community, to inspire others to deal with issues and challenges, to have hopes and dreams, and to believe that they can make a difference.

"Mike has always looked toward the future," Rick states. "So it's consistent then that he would be highly involved in helping the next generation that gets injured and dreaming about a cure. His whole life has been focused on helping improve people's lives."

౸౸

Mike's experience with his injury has led him to be ever more optimistic about the future. Like Rick, he's excited by the possible benefits of stem cell research for future generations of spinal injury patients—an area of research that many scientists believe will eventually allow us to regrow a severed spinal cord.

"The training I benefited from wasn't there when Rick Hansen had his accident or he wouldn't be in a wheelchair," Mike says. Today, about 70 percent of people with a spinal cord injury do have some level of recovery compared with about 30 percent back when Rick was injured in the seventies. As Rick points out, the possibility of a cure for spinal injuries is now a part of every research scientist's vocabulary. "Twenty years from now—with the research that Rick and others are doing—we may be able to repair the spine like a broken ankle," enthuses Mike. "One way or another, it's going to happen."

Rick agrees that with help from people like Mike we can build on the present for an even brighter future: "Today, there are not only specialized care centres like the one at VGH but imaging technology and drug therapy as well. The rehabilitation protocols are improving, and there's also been an explosion of progress in terms of inclusion into society. Attitudes have really improved.

"In the next thirty years or so, dreams we could have never even remotely imagined are poised to come true," he says. "So Mike's involvement at a time when leadership is required—when we need more people with spinal cord injuries engaged in setting priorities and adding value to the cause—couldn't come at a more opportune time. We're on the threshold of an unbelievable acceleration of change. "

~~~

Ask Rick Hansen to give you a mini-history lesson on the progress of attitudes and advances in the world of spinal cord injuries and you begin to realize why he appreciates having someone like Mike on his team.

"Prior to 1938, if you had a spinal cord injury, you usually didn't survive," explains Rick. "Most doctors thought there wasn't a lot of hope even if you did manage to survive. You'd probably spend years in a hospital. There was no rehab nurse, no knowledge about how to treat the spine, and no accessibility to the community. Attitudes were very paternalistic and negative.

"When I came along, 35 years later, there had been a fair bit of progress," he adds. "By 1973, there was knowledge on how to stabilize and treat spinal injuries. And a frontline generation of people had gone out into the community and started to create some levels of awareness and some levels of access. They were starting to create things like specialized rehabilitation centres."

However, plenty of misconceptions and obstacles still remained. "When I was injured, the chances of any kind of small recovery at all—movement in a finger, say—were about 30 percent," he reveals. "It was pretty much accepted that you wouldn't have a family, you wouldn't be able to walk again, and you wouldn't be able to hold out much hope for a career. The mindset was, Don't get your expectations high because you don't want to get disappointed."

❦

Mike and Rick kept in touch in the years immediately after the Wheels in Motion World Tour. "We kept running into each other at various public forums," Rick recalls. "I always had a great deal of respect for him. I've found him to be a people's leader with a great sense of humour. You never got the sense that he had an air about him. And he always had time for me. I was impressed by that."

When Mike was premier, Rick came up with the idea of creating a motivational program in schools that stressed the importance of a positive attitude in coming to terms with a disability. "Coaches and teachers have helped me to transfer the things I learned in sports to life," says Rick. "They really encouraged me to believe that my injury was only a temporary setback. They helped me realize that it was actually an opportunity. Because of that profound experience, I wanted to take those life lessons into the BC school system and create a life skills program."

For Rick, the program provided an opportunity to take some of his own experiences and let others benefit from them. In some ways, the program is a natural extension of his many visits to hospitals, where he would have conversations with young people whose lives were permanently changed by spinal trauma.

"Having been in that circumstance and having people come into my life and encourage me along the way, I understand that I can have an impact," he says. "However, I also recognize that you never know where the impact will come from and what sorts of dialogue might prove to be relevant. Everybody is different. They all come at things from a different perspective.

"So I just come into it with the intent to inspire them a little bit in terms of the determination to overcome an obstacle," says Rick. "You can't change that fateful moment when an accident happens. But you *can* change your attitude about the circumstances."

Like Mike, Rick believes a positive attitude and the ability to set realistic goals are important. Still, the road to a fulfilling recovery also means accepting certain limitations. "People should get as much recovery as they can," he advises. "And then, there are certain things that you have to willingly surrender. After that, it's a matter of not letting the disability diminish you."

As it turned out, Rick knew that his own views matched Mike's closely. "I thought what better person to talk to than Mike?" he explains. "Mike has a strong belief in a sense of community, empowerment, and youth. I was talking to him about the idea and he got pretty inspired."

Mike's conviction was fuelled by the fact that as a teacher Beckie could see the good Rick was doing in schools first-hand. "I was in the audience when Rick would speak to teachers," says Beckie. "He's so inspirational. There are some people who just get the message across and show you what real human spirit is and what it can do. Rick is one of those people."

Today, the program has proved so successful that it's being implemented in hundreds of schools across

Canada, but, initially, some provincial bureaucrats felt reluctant about testing the program in a couple of BC schools. This time around, Mike didn't have to put up with skeptical members. He used his influence to push the idea through. "There are certain times when you have to exercise a premier's prerogative to get things done," Mike remarks. "And this was one of those times."

꽈ꭴꭹꞈ

Rick says that he finds Mike's experience inspiring because it's a textbook example of how things can work out for the best. "If you look at Mike's story, it's like a best practice case study for how to treat spinal cord injury. Our intent is to take a look at what worked for people like Mike and make them the standard of care across the country.

"Every person with a spinal cord injury should have the ability to be 'medi-vaced' out rapidly and treated promptly at the scene in order to get stabilized," Rick opines. "They should also go to the best spinal cord injury centre. Unfortunately, those two things are not guaranteed, and the consequences of not being treated at the rapid rate by the right people at the right time can mean the difference between having recovery or not.

"On the other hand, if we just solved the problem in those two areas, the incidences of neurological impairment could be reduced by at least 40 percent, not to mention the further cost of complications in emotional health."

Like Mike, Rick believes in building on these two elements with the third strategy of spinal cord research. "Combined with more clinical trials on things like regrowth strategies and how to prevent the cord from being injured once it's damaged, we could probably see a reduction in neurological impairment by about 50 percent within two years," he says.

But, for Rick, Mike's example goes beyond what he can do for spinal cord research. As he points out, Mike is furthering the cause of spinal cord issues simply by living his life to the fullest along his path to recovery. "People can recognize through Mike's example that you don't have to be cured in order to be whole," Rick observes. "You can live with dignity, purpose, and meaning in spite of the fact that you may have a disability."

For Mike, living with a purpose means continuing to pursue the issues he has always valued. "I'm very grateful to still be engaged in the things that have always had meaning to me," he says about life after his accident. "I've learned that you can still catch your dreams." And as Mike was about to find out, there were still a few important dreams within his grasp.

8

HELL-BENT ON SUSTAINABLE CITIES

"He [Mike] loves the concept of sustainable cities so much that he'll talk about it twenty-four hours a day.... Sometimes, I just have to tell him, 'Stop! I don't want to spend our whole life talking about cities.'"
— BECKIE HARCOURT

A few months after Mike's accident, reporters asked him whether he might return to elected office. A recovering Mike jokingly told the same journalists who had once hounded him during the Bingogate affair, "I never thought I'd be so thankful to be standing in front of the scrum of the earth once again." Referring to his sky-rocketing popularity, reporters teased him about a return to politics. He quipped, "Beckie would push me off the cliff herself and not bother to pull my head out of the water." But on a more serious note, he now says, "I'd never go back to politics. I've found a way of doing what needs to be done without all the hassle."

As Mike wrote at the conclusion of his book *A Measure of Defiance*, "I retired from elected politics because I had fulfilled my personal commitment. But I am not going gently into anyone's good night. There are many things to do. My light is not anywhere near dying. There is a sustainable world out there to help organize."

Those words—written in the mid-1990s as Mike looked forward to "the second half of life's challenges," unaware of the many struggles that lay ahead—take on a new poignancy in light of his accident. But the man that *Vancouver Sun* political columnist Vaughn Palmer calls "a planner at heart" isn't about to give up on his passion for making cities live up to their future potential.

"I keep chugging along on the same agenda," he says with a laugh when asked about his continuing commitment to such issues as sustainability, the environment, and aboriginal rights. He may joke about an aversion to politics. However, the truth is some form of public service will always be in his blood. It's just taken a different form in recent years.

"I've been very fortunate to get a triple Ph.D. at the taxpayer's expense so to speak," he remarks. "If it weren't for the experience I've been able to gain over the years, I wouldn't be doing all these things on the scale and scope I am now, so giving back as much as I can just makes sense."

⌀⌀⌀

Mike has found that his focus on disability issues has been able to increase despite the demands of his rehabilitation. "I don't have to absorb the stress that comes with running a city or a province, so the ability to focus on implementing the ideas I really care about doesn't suffer from any distractions."

Mike claims to be only half joking when he explains the difference between his years in elected office and now. "Before I had power and immense aggravation," he says. "Now I have influence and no responsibility. People can accept my advice or not and I can just be an active citizen. For me, it's the best of both worlds."

Since leaving elected office, Mike has served on numerous boards. In 1996, the prime minister appointed him to the National Round Table on the Environment and the Economy (an independent body reporting directly to the PM), where he chaired the urban sustainability program. More recently he has served on a number of boards that focus on his passion for improving the quality of cities—he is a senior associate of the University of British Columbia's Liu Centre for the Study of Global Issues as well as the university's Sustainable Development Research Institute. Mike has also served as chair of UBC's International Centre for Sustainable Cities and vice-chair of the university-affiliated cities[PLUS] project.

Mike's commitment to all these projects can be measured by the fact that he remained involved in them to the best of his ability while recuperating in hospital and undergoing rehabilitation. His personal challenges tended to mesh with the broader social challenges he's stayed engaged in as a social activist, and staying active in such issues as sustainable cities was the best possible medicine for a competitive guy like Mike. In fact, the competitive element always brought out the best in him no matter how he was feeling.

In his role with cities[PLUS], many of the environmental and urban principles that Mike cherishes have been put to a fascinating test. The cities[PLUS] team (a partnership that included the Greater Vancouver Regional District, UBC's Liu Centre for the Study of Global Issues, the International Centre for Sustainable Cities, and the environmental planning firm The Sheltair Group, as well as other organizations) took part in a worldwide competition that had been organized by the International Gas Union in 2001-02, before Mike's accident. The team included leader Sebastian Moffatt of The Sheltair Group—along with fellow Sheltair Group members Elisa Campbell, Jane McRae, Lourette Swanepoel, and Lyle Walker. Other members of the team included Ken Cameron of the Greater Vancouver Regional District, Nola-Kate Seymoar of the International Centre for Sustainable Cities, and Loyd Axworthy of UBC's Liu Centre.

The gold medal would go to the city that best demonstrated a cohesive one-hundred-year strategy for sustainable development. Seventeen entries from all over the world were winnowed down to a short-list of nine cities, which ranged from San Diego to Berlin.

Vancouver was Canada's choice. The project lay close to Mike's heart, both intellectually and emotionally.

"The basic question was, How do you take the medium-term strategy of the regional district of Vancouver, which projected into the next twenty-five years, and stretch it to one hundred years?" explains Mike. To answer that question, the cities^{PLUS} team drew on the expertise of more than five hundred local experts—everyone from architects and engineers to environmental activists and business people.

The project investigated a number of issues that the regional district of Vancouver would face into the next century. They included everything from climate change and technological transformations to the problems of resource scarcity and globalization. These problems were dealt with in a manner that stressed both quality of life and environmental responsibility.

As vice-chair, Mike saw his primary job as getting the diverse personalities to work together toward a common goal. This did not always prove easy, which is why he spent considerable time on the phone smoothing things over from his hospital bed. "I would describe some of the people on the project as brilliant but a little prickly," observes Mike. "I just wanted to see it come together, so it was like, What's the end goal and how do we get there?"

Because of his spinal cord injury, Mike could not join his cities^{PLUS} colleagues for the international awards ceremony in Tokyo in June 2003. The flight would have been too arduous. But, much to his delight, he was rewarded with the news that the Vancouver proposal had won the gold medal. "Much sake was consumed that night," he grins, including a round for the purpose of toasting Mike.

Why did the Vancouver proposal win? "We used a model based on a real city of two million people," explains Mike, who credits the project's success to engaging a variety of professionals from the community. "It wasn't some fantasy design that was just put together by a bunch of academics and planners. It was based on real challenges and the solutions were going to be applied to the regional district."

As always, Mike took pride in the fact that the team offered eminently practical solutions to the increasingly difficult problem of urban growth. "I believe that innovative long-term planning can lead to a true renaissance in urban thought and action," he told reporters after the win. "Cities are all about choices, choices that become reality very quickly with lasting consequences. Over the twenty-first century—the urban century— much will depend upon getting the choices right."

Some of the right choices outlined in the cities[PLUS] project include a number of conservation concerns that every urban area will have to confront in the future. They include such "green" issues as water conservation, solar heating, and maximum use of recycling programs to a point where close to 100 percent of garbage is recycled in some way.

❦❦❦

Mike's latest commitment to progressive urban development involves an early 2004 appointment by Prime Minister Paul Martin. His role is to act as chief adviser on the PM's "new deal" for cities under Minister of State for Infrastructure and Communities John Godfrey. As the chair of a fifteen-member committee appointed by the prime minister, Mike will draw on his expertise about sustainable cities. Together, he and the other committee members will form cohesive strategies for an array of problems ranging from crime to urban gridlock.

"One of the massive issues that we're not dealing with very well is what I call the urban tsunami," says Mike. "It's the tidal wave of urban and population growth. This is especially true in developing countries, but Canada is no different."

Of Canada, he adds, "Seventy years ago, we used to be a largely rural population where only 20 percent of us lived in cities. Now, within the next decade, 90 percent of Canadians will be living in cities."

By 2015, there will be a drop in Canada's population due to a declining birth rate, but that decline will be made up for by increased immigration rates that will contribute another five million people within the next thirty years. "Ninety percent of that immigration will be going to five major urban centres that include Montreal, Toronto, and Vancouver," says Mike. "How are we going to deal with them?"

Along with this shift in population, three-quarters of the jobs are now in cities. "Canada has a huge advantage over other countries because we have this huge land mass with natural resources," Mike notes. "In the coming years, natural resource economies are going to be desperately needed globally."

He observes that in the future Canada will have a major advantage over other countries. "We have two dynamic economies—the urban knowledge-based high-tech sector and the natural-resource sector. Both of them are going to be very hot."

What does this mean for Canada? "We need to have healthy prosperous cities, both in large urban areas and smaller rural and aboriginal communities," he explains. "But the range of services that people expect from cities can no longer be handled by property tax. We're talking about things like the drug problem, the homeless, street kids. That's why we need a new deal for cities."

The "new deal" program intends to focus on a long-term plan for more liveable cities that addresses deeply ingrained urban problems. "Money's important to deal with these problems," says Mike. "But we need more than money. There needs to be a transition strategy for sustainability—a way to deal with things like our reliance on the car and urban sprawl. It's not like turning on a light switch. It won't happen overnight."

And yet, as difficult as the transition to sustainability is, Mike feels Canada has no choice. "Being sustainable means being competitive," he believes. "If we're not, we're simply going to languish and fade away. Our major Canadian cities need to be sustainable because they're gateways for close to 80 percent of the trade in Canada. That means creating an infrastructure and transportation system that gives us the ability to move around with maximum efficiency."

∽∼∾

The Martin appointment is just the latest indication that Mike may well be spending his sixties as a kind of elder statesman for the Gortex generation, someone who can seamlessly blend the modern concerns of the socially and culturally aware citizen into a clear, practical picture that makes sense. Typically, Mike sees his participation as a lifelong commitment. Not even spinal cord injury could stop his need to stay engaged in the issue of sustainable cities for long.

Beckie smiles, saying that Mike's interest in sustainable cities is so great that sometimes he needs to be reminded to stop thinking about it. "Michael can get very extreme on the projects he's working on," she confides. "He loves the concept of sustainable cities so much that he'll talk about it twenty-four hours a day. It's such a big part of his life that I see myself as needing to provide some balance." She laughs, adding, "Sometimes, I just have to tell him, 'Stop! I don't want to spend our whole life talking about cities.'"

All joking aside, Beckie is proud of her husband's drive to keep working on issues that he became involved in at the beginning of their marriage. "There's been a natural progression from his days on city council," she remarks. "It just has a wider impact these days. But all the things he's involved with now are issues he's always believed in.

"The thing that I find quite incredible is that he's making more of an impact now than when he was in elected office," she adds. "You would think that his time as mayor and premier would be the pinnacle of his career, but, in retrospect, I don't think so."

As Mike relates, he has no intention of stopping. "I'm going to be doing these kinds of things forever," he says of his desire to continue building better communities. "I think retirement's a phony concept. I was involved eighty or ninety hours a week as a storefront lawyer and a politician. Now I'm working half time at forty to fifty hours a week engaged in the issues that I feel passionate about. I didn't retire. I just changed gigs. I think that's important for your own sense of well-being.

"I stay engaged because I have a passion for these issues," he says of his life after leaving the premier's office. "I had absolutely no interest in joining a law firm.... Not to mention that there wasn't exactly an overwhelming number of offers to serve on the boards of banks and corporations," he quips.

⚮

Some people may be surprised by how much force Mike can bring to his social convictions. While he has used his characteristic grit and toughness to overcome the challenges posed by his spinal cord injury, he's best known as a master in the fine art of political compromise. His reward? "I've seen a lot of good ideas actually happen," he says. "It's not enough to have a good policy if it just sits there gathering dust. You've got to make it come alive by influencing others to make the changes and do the transformation."

But, as he points out, his tolerance for other points of view shouldn't be considered a weakness. "I'm prepared to give someone a chance if they make a mistake," he states. "But trying to take advantage of my good nature isn't the best idea.

"I've always wanted to do good things," he adds. "That's why politics has been a kind of instinct from early on. I knew that it was a way to put my values into action. And I was always getting thrown into it. My grade seven class elected me class president and I was involved in some form of student politics throughout high school, becoming school president in my final year."

He still remembers the value of his first steps in organized politics. "That's where I started to learn about the political process," he says. "I learned how to chair meetings and how to set goals."

His experience in high school gave him a respect for the political process and helped sharpen his social conscience. Mike's mind was also broadened by travel. In 1963, as a young university student, he went travelling around the Pacific. This trip had a great impact on his developing beliefs. "That's when I saw the impact of nuclear war, standing at ground zero in Nagasaki," he recalls. "It was a very tough experience."

"I remember going through this fishing village and seeing all the refugees going through Hong Kong," he says. "A grandfather and his grandchild were rummaging through the garbage piles looking for whatever they could find. I never forgot that."

As a student, he adamantly opposed the war in Vietnam. "They called me Ho Chi Harcourt in law school," he explains with a smile. "I felt it was the wrong war. I'm not a pacifist. I would have fought in the Second World War as my dad did."

Despite his passionate opposition to the Vietnam War, he rejected the era's radical politics immediately. "I remember going to a meeting of the Marxist-Leninists just out of curiosity," he says. "They kept saying there was going to be a revolution in Quebec by 1972 and in the rest of Canada by 1975. It was just nonsense. I thought, I'm outta here.

"I made the decision to become an activist before I went into law school," he remarks. "I figured the only way you were going to bring change in a democratic society like Canada is by becoming politically active. I wanted to find the right way for me to get things done as a peaceful but forceful activist, so I decided to learn the rules of the democratic legal system and change the rules."

The philosophy of being a peaceful but forceful activist carried through in Mike's political career. As mayor, he set up city-wide peace marches in the early

1980s. "I remember Beckie and I pushing Justen in a stroller across the Burrard Street Bridge," he smiles. "I nearly put out my back pushing that stroller. But 125,000 people showed up for the peace walk. It was really something."

∽∼∾

Even a tolerant guy like Mike has his limits, though. "The practical concept of freedom is called liberty," he says. "That doesn't mean doing whatever you want to do if it harms someone else. We should all be enlarging our lives without diminishing others, but it doesn't always happen that way."

Mike received an early lesson in this fact of life where a lot of kids are first tested—in his own neighbourhood. "When I was six, I was playing with a bunch of kids that included a Jewish friend of mine," he says. "One of the kids called him a dirty Jew. I said, 'You can't call my friend that.' He did it again, so I beat him up."

"I've never liked bullies," Mike explains. "I have always been very pugnacious about dealing with them in all forms, from racists to corporate bullies. I don't think you can deal with issues you care about by using passive resistance. You have to take those issues on, whether you're talking about defending the rights of First Nations people or the poor and abused."

∽∼∾

Not surprisingly, his interest in sustainable development took seed while Mike was investigating the nuts and bolts of becoming a storefront lawyer. Like many aspects of his life, it was an early example of how many of his passions ultimately converged to form a solid whole.

"My fascination with cities became a focus when I got out of university, he recalls. "I really didn't study urban geography or urban issues. But then I got into community law, which is based on the US model of inner-city ghettos from back in the days of President Lyndon Johnson's war on poverty. At the heart of the system was the idea of a full-time office with lawyers, paralegals, and others specializing in legal issues affecting the poor.

"In second-year law, I went down to Seattle with a criminal law professor from the University of British Columbia named Jerome Atrens," he says. "We were both intrigued by how the American model of the legal services program could be applied to Canada. "

Mike learned quickly that most lawyers focused on representing landlords rather than tenants, creditors rather than debtors, and government bureaucracies rather than the injured or unemployed worker looking for the basics. "The legal system is top heavy with lawyers representing those that are rich and powerful," he remarks. "Except for charitable resources and volunteer lawyers, there's a scarcity of resources to represent those who don't have influence.

"We wanted to flip that so that we became experts and were able to build that expertise into the law school and legal advice clinics," he explains. "The idea was to engage a whole series of volunteer lawyers to help those law students and clinics develop a legal aid and community law system, so that poor people got representation when they were in court on a criminal charge or a family matter."

While attempting to apply the US model to Vancouver, Mike understood that he and his colleagues faced at least one key difference. "We didn't have a ghetto," he says. "We had Main and Hastings and what would become known as the Downtown Eastside, but low-income people with the kind of problems we had to address were spread all over the city. So we had to improvise by utilizing neighbourhood houses, citizen action groups, and storefront information centres all over the place."

From there, Mike's fascination with cities grew throughout his political career. One writer referred to Mike as "the man who helped save Vancouver from the wrecking ball." Today, he's proud of the political decisions that have had a lasting effect on the place he calls home. "Allan Fotheringham used to describe Vancouver as the most beautiful setting in the world in search of a city," Mike notes. "While we've still got some issues to address, the city's managed to catch up to the setting. That's because of conscious choices we've made."

～～～

Mike's experience with both his injury and the subsequent rehabilitation continues to impact the way he feels about life. For Mike, the larger social issues of conservation and sustainable cities ultimately come down to how they affect people he's met in all walks of life.

Continue with this train of thinking and you might end up considering the details of conservation issues that Mike believes all urban areas should be starting to address now—"green" issues outlined in the cities^{PLUS} project, such as water conservation, solar heating, and recycling.

Mike is particularly interested in the way the precious resource of water is used in the average household. He points out that only 35 percent of Canadian municipalities meter water. Much of it is simply going to waste. "People basically have free use of water," he observes. "Whether they use it very sparingly or squander it. The first step is for people to realize that water is a limited resource, so we have to change our thinking about it.

"Then what you can do is start rethinking the way that we use and treat water," he adds. "We treat 100 percent of the water as though we're going to drink it, but probably less than 1 percent of the water that people use in their house is used for drinking. The rest is used for things like washing your dishes, watering your lawn, or for flushing the toilet."

Mike explains that it's unnecessary to build huge water-treatment plants to avoid the possibility of people drinking polluted water when less than 1 percent is used for consumption. The cities^{PLUS} solution to this problem involved employing a cascading water system as a transition measure to sustainability. Simply put, it's a method where the spillover from your drinking water goes into your dishwasher or your clothes washer. From there, it goes into your toilet to be used as flushing water. Then, the water can be processed through a charcoal filter to water your lawn or wash your car.

"We can eliminate 90 percent of the water that we use by employing the same water in a multitude of ways," says Mike, who'd like to see people get used to recycling water in the same way they've become familiar with the process of recycling bottles or newspapers. "It's a whole new way of thinking about a very scarce resource," he adds.

Mike points out that the same common sense approach can be applied to household energy conservation. Apart from elements like insulation and double-glazed windows, he believes that solar heating will inevitably become an efficient and practical way to heat your water, for example. "Fifty percent of the energy that people use in their houses goes for hot water," he explains. "So if you can get that solar energy happening, it will cut down your hydro bill dramatically."

He feels that it's just a matter of time before solar energy technology and other methods of conservation will progress to the point where they are working for all of us: "Instead of consuming energy, you'll eventually be able to turn your house into a place where you're not only fulfilling your energy needs but creating a surplus of energy."

As Mike explains, it's not only a question of waiting for the technology to do the work for us. It's also a question of developing a more environmentally friendly attitude in your daily routine—whether that means maintaining a rooftop vegetable garden or maximizing the recycling of family garbage. "It wasn't that long ago that we thought nothing of placing all of our garbage in a dump," he observes. "Now approximately 50 percent of our garbage is being recycled in some way. Someday that percentage will be closer to doubling."

∾⌒∾

Mike considers the 1960s opposition to Vancouver's proposed freeway a turning point in the way cities chose to look at the future. "It was a rejection of the car and freeway approach and, in doing so, it embraced the spirit of communities," he says. "It was something that started to happen all across Canada. We didn't want to have freeways destroy the integrity of cities like they have in places like Los Angeles."

Not that Canada is a transportation paradise. Mike explains, for example, that traffic flow is still far from ideal for the average Toronto commuter, despite a transit system that's a definite step in the right direction.

Even with such ongoing concerns of modern traffic congestion, the early struggle to reject the car and freeway approach has sparked a wave of community participation across the country that has lasted to this day, a feeling that as Mike puts it, "important decisions didn't have to be left in the hands of political bureaucrats. We could stop the urban renewal craziness."

"A lot of things were really put right in Vancouver in the seventies and eighties," he adds. "But there are still these huge issues that revolve around understanding the needs of cities." He points out that Vancouver's World Urban Forum—a conference that will bring together experts on sustainable development in June of 2006—is an important step toward resolving some of those issues. For Mike, the forum is another opportunity for goal-setting. "We need to have things reasonably developed by then," he says.

He uses the example of creating a much-needed complete transportation system linked to denser urban land use and a modern transit line. Specifically Vancouver's Richmond-Airport-Vancouver (RAV) Rapid Transit Project, which he supports with a characteristic mixture of passion and common sense. "I'm engaged in getting the RAV line built so that it creates a less car-oriented, clogged, and polluted city. That's the kind of city that I want to see happen for my son and his children. But it also has the benefit of creating an alternative for people who can't afford a car."

Mike views his involvement in this project as a perfect example of how he's always sought to make his personal and political beliefs an integral part of the same objective. "If you can enhance the quality of your own life while creating a positive spin-off on other people, so much the better," he says. "Social activism has taught me that you can integrate what matters to you personally with a broader scope of accomplishments that are going to help future generations."

After so many years of integrating his personal beliefs with this activism, he's well aware of the personal rewards. "To a certain extent, you can say it's a selfish thing to do because it makes you feel good to go after these larger goals," he remarks. "But so what? It's also an important thing to do."

∽∼∾

Mike travelled to many different cities in his old Plan A life. While he firmly believes in the power of local governments to improve their communities, his political career also offered the opportunity to see the concept of sustainable cities in a global context. It was one of his last official acts as premier—a trip to Pakistan, India, and Indonesia—that galvanized his desire to do more to promote the idea of sustainable cities.

"Our flight to New Delhi from Mumbai had the prime minister and seven premiers on board as well as five hundred business people," he says. "We were the number one plane slated to land, but they just couldn't do it. We had to circle the airport for two hours because the air pollution was so bad there was inadequate visibility."

In New Delhi, Mike visited a shantytown of 100,000 people. "They had a well about every hundred yards," he recalls. "Their houses were just makeshift shacks built from whatever they had managed to scrounge.

Right beside them, there were these big villas surrounded by huge walls."

Mike was still trying to assimilate the chaos he had seen on the streets of Mumbai. "There were masses of beggars with no limbs," he recalls. "They were pushing their way through traffic on little carts and begging for money. It was really dangerous for them. I remember being horrified."

The view from his Mumbai hotel room did not seem much more encouraging. "You could see a section of sky that was sort of blue and then a grey layer in the mid-third of your vision," he says. And then you would look down at the polluted water.... It was just a mass of pollution from the ground up to where you could see a bit of blue sky."

In 1996, shortly after leaving the premier's office, Mike attended the Habitat conference in Istanbul. The visit came close enough on the heels of the trip to India to prove especially alarming. "I just saw masses of poverty and terrible air pollution," he recalls. "I realized just how horrific the whole urban growth situation was becoming," he says. "Things had gotten so much worse internationally since the original Habitat conference, which had taken place in Vancouver in 1976.

"With most of the cities in developing countries, you couldn't breathe the air," he adds. "There was huge growth in the urban slums, massive poverty, and inadequate urban governments. Things were just going from bad to worse. Less was being done for cities and, at the same time, the world population was expanding.

"Seventy percent of the pollution in oceans comes from pollution in adjacent urban areas on the coastal seas," he notes. "A lot of the climate change that is happening is man-made from air pollution in cars and vehicles as well as the coal fire and energy plants from industry. The rampant using up of natural resources such as water is because of the rapid growth of cities," he says.

As Mike points out, the economic and social problems caused by unfettered urban growth continue to be a desperate problem in various cities around the world. "A quarter of a million Mexico City residents are coming out [of the country] en masse in 2004 because of the rampant kidnappings that have filtered down into the lower reaches of the middle class," he says. "Who wants to live like that?"

North Americans, he says, cannot afford to be complacent. "Our cities are starting to fall apart too," he observes. "Our water systems are falling apart, our transportation systems are inadequate. There's homelessness, drugs, and an increase in aboriginal issues and challenges. The rate of poverty is increasing.

"If we don't act quickly our cities are going to turn into hellholes," he says bluntly. "They're going to be places where you can't breathe the air and the water will be polluted. In developing countries, there will be the potential of cholera or typhoid outbreaks. The middle class and rich will have to live in compounds behind barbed wire and armed guards while the poor live in crime-ridden slums."

❦

The Istanbul experience spurred Mike on to become re-engaged with the University of British Columbia's Sustainable Development Research Institute. He began to do interviews and speaking engagements, coining that phrase "urban tsunami" to express his fear of what would happen globally unless we banded together to make the necessary changes in planning and lifestyle.

"The urban tsunami was getting ready to crash down on us in the next twenty-five years," he explains. "The growth from 6 billion people—half of them living in cities for the first time in human history—to 8.5 billion is a definite factor. By and large, 2.4 billion of the next 2.5 billion people will be living in the cities of developing countries." "I just saw that if we didn't get our cities right, we were going to have horrific problems as a species," he observes. "It wasn't just the terrible dilemma for human beings, but the impact it was having on the environment. We were consuming the world's resources beyond the natural capacity of the environment to cope with it."

❦

When Mike was asked to bring his skills to the table as chair of the prime minister's External Advisory Committee on Cities and Communities, he felt eager to contribute. Part of his mandate is to expand our notion of how cities and communities function. "We're going to broaden the concept of sustainable cities in a number of ways," he explains. "First of all, the conventional view of sustainable cities is that you have a vibrant economy, a healthy environment—clean air, clean water, edible food, biodiversity being protected."

Mike's approach takes this view one step further. "The healthy community idea should also address such social justice issues as the drug and crime problem," he says. "Instead of a three-legged stool of sustainability— economic, environmental, and social—we're saying it should be a four-pillar approach. We're adding in a cultural context.

"The approach involves a long-term vision where the financial resources are in place to make sure that the infrastructure—sewer, water, waste management, and transportation—are brought up to speed. It's about a better relationship between the voters and government."

The plan involves spending billions of dollars over the next decade to tackle various urban problems while improving the infrastructure of cities. Mike explains that the changes will be "big, bold, and quick," with a major factor being the elimination of red tape between the various levels of government. "We've been given the mandate by Prime Minister Martin to think outside of the box," he says. "Not just for the big cities but for the small, remote, and aboriginal communities as well."

In light of the fact that 80 percent of Canadians now live in cities, with the number bound to increase to 90 percent in the coming years, Mike says: "The national government is massively involved in our cities and communities anyway, so the real issue is how they're going to be involved. Are they going to be involved in a stupid, uncoordinated, unco-operative way, or are they going to be involved in an intelligent, co-operative way where a bunch of complementary issues link up?"

Mike wants a number of coordinated initiatives to be linked up in order to ensure that the government is practising sustainability at a grassroots level. "It's called horizontality," he says. "There are environmentally friendly cleaning products you can use to clean public buildings and environmentally friendly vehicles you can use to run government fleets. There are a lot of things that can work together to make practical sense."

What does the future hold if everything goes smoothly? "I'd like to see Canada be thought of around the world as the country that got its cities right first," Mike states, As he explains, a fresh approach to the future of our cities will reap healthy economic benefits across the country: "The link between being sustainable and being economically competitive is increasingly more apparent. People just won't invest in a city that's unattractive, much less send their key employees to work there, so your economy will inevitably do badly if you're not sustainable."

⌘

While Mike is clearly applying his talents to a bigger canvas than he used to, a common thread has always run through his social activism. He often says that his career has been a happy combination of conviction and serendipity, and so there are times when he's quite surprised by how the dots of his past, present, and future can connect with such unexpected grace. It may sound ironic for someone who continues to recover from a serious spinal injury. But, for Mike, the old saying, "What goes around, comes around" holds absolutely no fear, maybe because what went around in the first place had so much goodwill behind it.

One example? In the mid-1960s, Mike chaired the Vancouver Youth Communications Centre Society. Popularly known as Cool Aid, the organization sought to provide social support to transient youth. Recently, it was discovered that years ago Cool Aid had placed money in a bank account and then forgotten about it. The deposit subsequently gathered interest for decades. To the surprise of Mike and others, the account contained twenty thousand dollars.

"We just plowed the money back into the inner-city schools," says Mike, of one of his favourite causes. And for a guy who can never forget the image of a little kid rummaging through a big city garbage can, that kind of synchronicity is a very cool thing.

9

PLAN B FOR THE PLANET

"If you have spirit, courage, and faith, you can help heal our tattered, battered planet."
— MIKE HARCOURT

After Mike had become used to the many adjustments he had to make following his accident, he was frequently asked to give speeches. Never one to shirk from talking about his favourite causes—among them, aboriginal issues, the environment, and Vancouver's winning bid for the 2010 Winter Olympics—he would take the podium with all the zeal of someone who was spreading a personal message, and his addresses would be greeted with enthusiasm.

Now that his own Plan B was working out, it almost seemed as if Mike had a Plan B for the planet at large, a politically holistic agenda he had developed as mayor and premier that he wanted to refine in his current role as an experienced adviser and social activist. It was a philosophy that would take advantage of his talent of drawing diverse people and issues together into a common agenda—whether it involved defending the underdog or finding a new way for a globally significant event like the Olympics to contribute to the social good.

His goal was simple and can be best expressed by a line he wrote for an address to a group of business executives. "If you have spirit, courage, and faith," he said, "you can help heal our tattered, battered planet."

ఇఇఇ

No part of the planet is more special to Mike than British Columbia. "British Columbia is one of the most ecologically diverse areas in the world," he says. It has six hundred different ecosystems. I defy you to go anywhere in BC and not be blown away by such spectacular diversity."

These are the words of someone who's had a lifelong love affair with the   province's landscape, which has in no way been lessened by what he jokingly refers to as his "swan dive at low tide."

"Before getting into politics, I toured the entire province in an old '62 Dodge Dart that I called the blue pig," he recalls. "I got a tremendous sense of the wonder and excitement that comes with our natural surroundings. Not just in the bigger cities but in the smaller towns as well. I defy anyone to experience British Columbia and not be totally blown away by the sheer beauty of the landscape. I've always felt that way and that feeling was constantly reinforced when I travelled as premier.

"I've had the good fortune to meet tens of thousands, if not hundreds of thousands of people who live in BC," he adds. "That's when you realize that the citizenry is every bit as magnificent as their surroundings. Having that experience makes preserving the environment even more important for future generations."

As a politician, Mike always believed in a coordinated approach to solving problems. This is especially true in a province like British Columbia where environmental policy has often suffered because of a three-way clash between logging interests, environmentalists, and aboriginal rights. The fact that so many important issues intersect at the point of how we should treat our natural world has never been lost on Mike.

"A healthy environment can't be separate and apart from social issues," he observes. "It's an integral part of the sustainability principle. You can't have a prosperous economy or a stable and just society without it. Everything has to be connected."

His long-standing belief in the fundamental principles behind aboriginal rights forms the cornerstone of his philosophy on the environment. "Before you can develop a long-term government strategy on what land to preserve or where to farm, you have to figure out how aboriginal land and crown title can peacefully co-exist in one territory." For Mike, settling the problems related to aboriginal rights is key to forging a new and lasting prosperity both in British Columbia and across the country. "Then we'll have peace in the land," he says. "But until we deal with these land use issues, we're going to have increasing violence, increasing boycotts of our products, and decreasing investment."

∽∾∾

Mike believes his spinal cord injury has heightened his capacity to seize the moment, not that he was particularly slow to do so in the first place. The way he became an adviser to the team that inevitably put together the successful bid for the 2010 Winter Olympics is a case in point—and an area where his ideas have grown in new directions since his accident.

Mike was en route to an Australian lecture tour in July of 2000 when, much to his surprise, he discovered that the key members of Vancouver's 2010 Olympics bid committee were on the same plane. "The whole Olympic brain trust was headed down to talk to the organizing committee of the Sydney Olympics about preparing for Vancouver's upcoming bid," he recalls. "They wanted to learn a few lessons from them."

Mike had been mayor during Vancouver's highly successful Expo 86, and the experience had taught him that such events can be effectively used to do more than simply revitalize a city's infrastructure. They can also have a positive long-term effect on citizens, the environment, and the tourism industry.

The first step is sound planning and fiscal management combined with shared financial responsibilities on all levels of government, a strategy that Mike put into place with Expo. Mike points out that that Expo 86, unlike Montreal's Expo 67 and the Summer Olympics of 1976, left many long-term benefits for

Vancouver. "It allowed us to accelerate a whole bunch of projects that should have been done anyway," he explains. "We cleaned up the north side of False Creek, built the new Cambie Bridge and—thanks to the persistence of Senator Jack Austin—got the cruise ship facility and conference centre down by the waterfront."

On board the plane to Australia, Mike's natural inclination to talk to anyone who happens to be next to him—whether he's on a plane or in a doctor's waiting room—soon took over, but this wasn't just a pleasant, rambling chat. Mike's positive experience with Expo had left him thinking of new ways to bolster the proposal for Vancouver's winning Olympic bid. "In isolation, the Olympics themselves are basically a sporting event," he remarks. "In terms of tourism, it's a golden egg for the Vancouver-Whistler area, plus all of BC, if it's done right. But, more importantly, the opportunity to use it as a social catalyst is huge."

Having done his homework on the Sydney Olympics, Mike decided to take advantage of the unexpected encounter to talk about sustainability. "Sydney was the first Olympics to actually incorporate the idea of being environmentally responsible," he explains. "It was the first games to go beyond sports and culture to include a whole series of thoughts on the environment. It cleaned up both the harbour and a toxic abandoned industrial site as well as expanding their transportation system."

Mike wanted to take the Sydney concept a step further to make Vancouver's bid the first true sustainability

Olympics. In addition to incorporating environmental initiatives, he wanted to take the unprecedented step of encompassing a variety of broader social-justice issues. This meant seeking advice from a wide range of local communities, which would include everything from aboriginal participation to the input of the Downtown Eastside.

As always, Mike had no hesitation about making a passionate pitch for sustainability. "I told them my idea and laid out all the issues I felt should be addressed in terms of Vancouver," he recalls. "There was a very robust dialogue about everything from the desperate need for lower- and middle-income housing to street kids who need apprentice and training programs if they're going to get off drugs."

As it turned out, Mike had plenty of time to develop a convincing argument. "We flew from Vancouver to Honolulu, and we got stuck there because of some delay in the connecting flight to Sydney," he remembers. "These guys couldn't get away from me. I had them captive for seventeen hours, so they had to listen to me."

Mike's persuasive argument to his captive audience paid off. "They were really good about it," he recalls. "They just latched on to the basic idea and decided to run with it."

As the plan for the winning bid was developed further, Mike would add a heartfelt concept that resulted directly from his spinal cord injury. It involved the inspired idea of using an Olympic-type medal system of gold, silver, bronze, and honourable mention as a way of rating how accessible participating cities were to the disabled community. While Mike is currently oversee- ing a process to help determine the criteria used in such a rating system, he stresses that the awards are es- sentially meant to be used as motivational tools.

"It's not a critical process in the sense of being highly judgmental," he says. "It's just a method to focus much-needed attention on the ways cities can be more successful in dealing with accessibility for the disabled."

~~~

It's not surprising that the activist in Mike sees the 2010 Olympics as another convenient opportunity for goal- setting, especially in terms of aboriginal rights. If the whole world is going to be watching British Columbia, then why not raise the bar a little higher in terms of so- cial justice? As a federally appointed member of the British Columbia Treaty Commission, Mike would like to use 2010 as a target date for resolving some long- standing aboriginal treaties.

"I'd like to see us have completed treaties with all the aboriginal people in the province in the next five to ten years," he says. "It would be the mark of having created a new relationship based on mutual respect and trust. The payoff would be a stable civil society, not only for British Columbians but [for] all people who want to invest here. A peaceful coexistence be- tween aboriginal title and crown title in the same territory is going to create a much healthier society."

Mike first became interested in aboriginal rights while studying the issue in law school. The more he investigated this issue, the more he became convinced of a deeply rooted injustice toward the aboriginal people, an injustice that was buried under a mountain of legalese.

"The official position in BC was that aboriginal rights didn't exist," he says. "If they *did*, they'd been extinguished by Confederation in 1871. And, if they did exist and *hadn't* been extinguished by Confederation, it was solely a federal responsibility." He shakes his head, adding: "That kind of straight-arming went all the way back to [nineteenth-century BC governor] Sir James Douglas when he ran out of money."

"It's that kind of attitude that allowed all these other racist things to happen," observes Mike. "If aboriginal people don't have any rights to begin with, then we can get rid of their language and their culture. We can crush them."

Mike paints a dismal picture of the lack of aboriginal rights. "The government basically said, 'If they want to sue us, throw them in jail,'" he explains. "'And, while you're at it, make sure any lawyer that works with them will be disbarred. We'll just put them on reserves, and when we need more of their land, we'll send out a commission to alter the boundaries for our commercial interests.'"

What Mike discovered in law school amounted to a politically sanctioned way to hold back generations of aboriginal young people in a Catch-22 of spiralling expectations. "The government threw their kids into residential schools from the age of five to fifteen," he says. "So why are we surprised that you've got dysfunctional aboriginal families? The parents didn't see their kids during their childhood. Where were they supposed to get the parenting skills?"

"You do this kind of thing for generations," he says. "You take away their religion, their language, their culture, and their rights as citizens. And then you basically say that they have to convert to our way of life. Is it any wonder there's a lack of self-worth? If you had a rotten miserable existence for so long, how are you going to respond?"

Mike's stance on the aboriginal issue is clear. He believes that the problems of the aboriginal people are deeply rooted in the way the government has treated them historically. Due to this fact, certain prejudices continue to be reinforced and encouraged. "The real solution is getting rid of the injustice and all the accompanying barriers," he says.

～～～

Mike's feelings about aboriginal rights ran so deep that they fuelled his desire to become involved in provincial politics. "I left my comfortable pew of the mayor's office in 1986 because I felt very strongly about the issue," he explains. "I got elected three times as mayor and probably could have gotten re-elected, but I saw that the aboriginal issue was eating away at the soul of

British Columbia. I felt that who we are was either going to be enhanced or diminished by our relationship with the aboriginal people."

By the time Mike had opened his storefront law office in the late 1960s, the Red Power movement was emerging across Canada. "The Trudeau government wanted to make assimilation happen and the aboriginal people revolted across the country," recalls Mike. "I started to see a lot of Red Power advocates down at my storefront law office. It became clear to me that it was in everybody's best interests for the First Nations to move from welfare reserves to being a self-governing, self-sufficient community."

Aboriginal rights were recognized under constitutional changes in the early 1980s. Despite this, things were heating up in BC, a fact that didn't escape Mike's attention. "There was still this denial under the Social Credit government of the time," he says. "I saw increasingly that it was leading to a much more destructive British Columbia."

Added to the potentially volatile mix of the aboriginal issue was the growing controversy between environmentalists and loggers. "British Columbia was spiralling into a confrontational society," recalls Mike. "There were battles going on over a hundred watersheds all over the province and the violence was beginning to accelerate. I saw that we were heading for disaster as a province if we didn't deal with this because we still depend a lot on natural resources.

"The reason I got into provincial politics was to create a new relationship between the aboriginal and non-aboriginal people through mutual understanding and negotiation rather than confrontation or litigation," he explains. "The foundation of that was the modern treaties based on the principles we outlined in the BC treaty process and commission."

But making headway on the issue proved frustrating, even after he became premier. "Aboriginal rights were considered too politically hot," he says. "Everyone was scared to touch it because they felt we wouldn't get elected." Mike was prepared to deal with stalling tactics on the issue from the right-wing opposition. What surprised him, however, was the amount of flack he got from his own party.

"The left wing refused to accept that crown land could have anything but crown title, which was for all the people," explains Mike. "As socialists, they didn't believe in special rights like aboriginal ownership, so for different ideological reasons, a lot of people in the NDP didn't want to deal with aboriginal rights.

"I thought they were both wrong," he adds. "So it was a real fight to overcome both sides. I felt the best way to deal with it was to develop a whole new approach to environmental issues in British Columbia." He did so by linking the issues of environmentalists, loggers, and the aboriginal peoples and looking for common ground. He was ultimately able to engineer a policy agreement.

"I started out with land use and park preservation, a new forest practices code, and the BC Treaty Commission," he recalls. "I got an environment and jobs accord with some basic goals in place. We were going to protect 12 percent of the province's wilderness areas, settle aboriginal titles, and move to a new, more ecologically viable way of practising forestry while creating more jobs."

As Mike explains, planning was essential. "We just basically zoned the province as to where people could do things like cut down trees, graze cattle, and mine," says Mike. "We made all those decisions without prejudice to aboriginal title. We wanted to redo land use planning with aboriginal rights in mind through treaties."

Over an eight-year period, Mike also managed to reach his goal of doubling the preservation of British Columbia's wilderness areas from 6 to 12 percent. The concept of protecting 12 percent of the unique wilderness areas of the world was one of the highlights of 1987's United Nations report *Our Common Future* and served as an inspiration to Mike.

❧

Mike's reputation as a fair and knowledgeable negotiator in the area of aboriginal rights continues to linger. Prior to his accident, he had been quietly working behind the scenes for three years at sorting out some of the Musqueam band's issues with its leaseholders. In 2003, he accepted a federal appointment to head the British Columbia Treaty Commission.

It's a measure of how committed Mike is to his work on the commission that it takes up about 50 percent of his working schedule. But he's clearly convinced that the ultimate goal is worth it. "In terms of the quality of your civil society and your democracy there are great moral benefits," he says. "It's just the right thing to do, which I think is always the best argument for doing anything.

"It was natural to carry on with the work I started in the premier's office," he explains. "Especially since I saw that we were labouring in the process that I had set in motion. We weren't moving as quickly or as well as I thought we should."

After many decades of government stalling, Mike's dedication led to a Nisga'a treaty agreement in principal in 1996. Leading up to this were such accomplishments as the creation of the BC Treaty Commission in 1992 and getting forty-four of the First Nations involved in the treaty settlement process in 1995.

Mike's family supported his commitment to aboriginal rights. For Justen, his father's commitment is a source of great pride. "I think one of the best examples of my dad sticking to his beliefs no matter what is the Nisga'a treaty settlement that he started when he was premier," says Justen. "He supported something that frightened a lot of voters because of the xenophobia over land claims. He pushed the treaty process not only because it was the right thing to do but because it would have lasting benefits for the Nisga'a, British

Columbia aboriginals, and all British Columbians."

Over the years, Mike has seen the lasting benefits from his work with the Nisga'a. He uses Terrace, a small town in the interior of British Columbia where the Nisga'a have started up a number of thriving businesses, as an example of how aboriginal settlements can benefit an entire community. As Mike observes, "People are saying, 'Thank God for the treaty,' in terms of the health and well-being of our local economy because the rest of the economy is suffering over the softwood lumber issue."

But, as Mike explains, treaty settlements also hold the promise of huge economic benefits. "As soon as I got into the premier's office, we had a report from Price-Waterhouse showing that $1 billion of investment per year was not coming into British Columbia because of the uncertainty and the risk of blockades," says Mike. "And it's still happening, so settlements hold the key to the largest mega-project we're ever going to see economically. It could account for a $100 billion to a $150 billion increase in the GDP in British Columbia over the next twenty years."

"The federal and provincial governments are going to put between $9 and $10 billion into treaties at an average of about $500 million a year," he adds. While those may sound like big numbers, Mike considers the investment a wise move. "The government is going to get that initial cost back ten to fifteen times over in the long term," he observes. "When you look at the big picture, it's a minor start-up cost."

The long-term math yields impressive results. Once the numbers sink in, it becomes clear why Mike calls settling aboriginal treaties "a combination of doing good and doing well." He explains that $10 billion will flow into the settlements over the next twenty years, most of that from federal coffers. With economic multipliers, the benefits will be at least $40 billion as the settlement resources flow into the aboriginal communities and the impediments to investment coming into the province are removed. With future economic benefits that amount could eventually double.

"It's going to take a while for the scars to heal and the prejudices to be overcome," says Mike. "It will take a couple of generations before First Nations people become self-governing and self-sufficient, but making an investment in the process is worth doing."

"It's an important part of maintaining the ecological integrity that we have in BC," he adds. "With all the massive urbanization happening around us, it's absolutely essential for us to be good stewards of all the ecological wonder that we have—whether it's the magnificent coastal rainforest or the desert around the South Okanagan.

But Mike's concern for wilderness preservation goes well beyond the borders of his home province. In recent years, he's been instrumental in developing a new North American Wilderness Strategy that encompasses both the United States and Canada. "Issues like land use planning, forestry, and protected-area strategy got me engaged with the Canadian Parks and Wilderness Society," he says. "We came up with a whole different approach to wilderness conservation called conservation biology."

Eventually, Mike hopes that this new and comprehensive method of wilderness conservation will be accepted around the globe. "The traditional approach was having a park here and a park there," says Mike. "You may have had protected areas, but the migratory corridors were not preserved to allow migratory species to travel between these islands of preservation. And, without these crucial paths, they could actually be viewed as islands of extinction."

As Mike explains, the concept of conservation biology deals less with islands of preservation than what he terms "networks of survival." It's an all-encompassing conservation strategy that preserves migratory pathways as well as encouraging logging practices that maintain a peaceful coexistence with the surrounding wildlife.

"Some work we did on the national roundtable on the conservation of nature led me into this collaborative work on the concept of the North American Wilderness Strategy," he says. "The philosophy behind it was to embrace the whole continent rather than breaking it up by dealing with a part here and a part there.

"Birds and monarch butterflies don't stop their flight at the Canadian border," he points out. "Wolves and bears don't know that they have to pass a customs shack and neither do the whales that are taking the huge migratory routes between the Bering Sea and the Baja.

"In order to preserve huge corridors like the Pacific Flyway for millions of birds that fly between North America and South America, you needed a holistic continental approach to these kinds of issues. If any one of their fuelling stations for water and food were interrupted anywhere along that corridor, it would lead to the extinction of the species."

Mike gives an example of the way environmental links can be found anywhere across North America. "If you lost the San Pedro River between Arizona and Northern Mexico, there would be drastic consequences," says Mike. "The cottonwoods in that area have insects which feed millions of birds along that Flyway. If you lost that river because of the lowering water table, that would kill the trees and the birds that need those trees to survive."

Mike notes that some see the North American Wilderness Strategy as slightly ahead of its time, but he feels that the program is simply embracing a new way of thinking, which rejects narrow viewpoints in favour of forming a vital relationship between different countries.

In May 2003, Mike received the prestigious James Harkin Medal for his tireless contribution to preserving British Columbia's wilderness. In his acceptance speech, Mike paid tribute to the vision of the BC conservationist, saying: "James Harkin got it right. He called for vast areas in which the beauty of the landscape is protected from profanation, the natural wildlife and plants preserved and the peace and solitude of primeval nature retained."

Mike went on to call for a continental movement to build networks of protection and link together a North American natural network within the next two decades. "I want to give Americans, Canadians, and Mexicans the opportunity to contribute to a transformation—one that will resonate through countless generations to come," he remarked.

At the time, Mike had no idea that he, too, was about to undergo a transformation through his spinal cord injury, nor had he yet reflected that it would take the same seemingly infinite amount of wisdom and courage to help heal our battered planet as it is taking to heal his own battered body. However, with the help of others, he would not only learn that lesson well but pass it on at every opportunity. To this day, the lesson continues to resonate.

10

CATCHING YOUR DREAM

"It doesn't matter whether you're dealing with bank-ruptcy, divorce, or a spinal cord injury. The potential for a better future is there, depending on your attitude."
— Mike Harcourt

With the passing of time, both Beckie and Mike continue to reaffirm many of their core values as a result of Mike's accident. They've also learned a few new and valuable lessons along the way. "Sometimes life says to you, 'Okay, Plan A is over. Get on with Plan B,'" says Mike. "And you know something? Beckie and I are enjoying Plan B more than we thought. It was a terrible accident, but I learned a lot. You can still catch your dreams. It's just different.

"In some bizarre, serendipitous way, the accident has transformed the success I've had in my life a thousand-fold," he notes. "I've discovered that what happened to me has had a profound and lasting effect on others. But other people have also inspired me."

A perennial list-maker, Mike couldn't resist the prospect of sharing ten lessons in life that he has learned as a result of his spinal cord injury. Most of them are things that he already knew in his heart. But, as he explains, "the accident has deepened and enriched my feelings about all these things. It's left me feeling that they're more important than ever."

LESSON ONE:
Life Is a Precious, Fragile Gift

"I've really learned to take nothing for granted," says Mike. "And that feeling was heightened by the accident. Every day it seemed as if there was something to be truly grateful for, whether it was getting off the antibiotics and being able to enjoy a glass of wine or learning how to negotiate the slick rocks on a path to the beach.

"The pleasure Beckie and I take in being able to enjoy the simple things is really wonderful," he adds. "Every day, we continue to be thankful for at least one thing that life has to offer."

LESSON TWO:
Bad Things Happen to Good People

During the rehabilitation process, Mike constantly saw people with spinal cord injuries who were simply victims of circumstance. But for Mike, the issue goes deeper than any specific physical disability. "A lot of people get stuck in Plan A and can't get out," he observes. "They think they're fated to a life they don't like, a job they hate, and a relationship that's going nowhere. They don't realize that they have choices, but those choices take courage. Part of that courage is accepting the fact that life isn't always fair. Only then can you begin to make changes."

LESSON THREE:
How You Live Your Life Is Key

"The way that you treat people has a direct bearing on the way that you feel about yourself," says Mike. "In my opinion, if you feel suspicious or expect the worst from people all the time, that's based on insecurity and a lack of self-worth.

"People have let me down," he observes. "The Dave Stupich, Bingogate stuff is a classic example of that. I've been disappointed by others, but nine times out of ten, I expect the best to happen and it usually does. It's just a lot easier living your life that way." "My dad's philosophy of life is pretty straightforward," says

Justen. "Live it the best way you can. He has a passion for everything he does. If he's not interested in something, he won't do it regardless of remuneration. To him, life isn't about how much money he makes or what people think of him. It's about doing the things you believe in and helping others."

Mike's passion for life extends to other areas as well. He uses the recent example of returning to the tennis court as Beckie's doubles partner. "We had to make all sorts of adjustments," he says. "I'm allowed two bounces now instead of one, but it doesn't matter. Getting back to it and doing the best you can is still fun."

Beckie remembers the first time they attempted a doubles game together. "We missed a whole lot of the balls because it hadn't registered in my mind that I would have to go after the ball," she recalls. "It's been a while since the accident, but, in my mind, I somehow thought that Mike would get the ball because that's what he always used to do. Now, I've got to get the ball unless it goes right to Mike.

"It's not the same tennis game," observes Beckie. "But, to me, that's not the point at all. It's Mike having what it takes to start the process again—to dress the part, get to the court, hold the tennis racket, and hit the ball back when it comes to him."

And yet, for all the adjustments, some important things haven't changed at all. "We still have a great time playing tennis and having drinks with our opponents afterwards," says Beckie. "It's a nice part of our life that we've managed to rebuild."

Today, Mike remains focused on reaching his goals with a rigorous health and fitness routine that includes his continuing commitment to physio, naturopathy, chi-gong, weight training, and work on the treadmill. "It's particularly important after a serious accident," he notes. "That old saying 'use it or lose it' is really true. For me, staying healthy and keeping as fit as I can is a lifelong promise that I've made to myself."

LESSON FOUR:
The Right Attitude toward Adversity Is Essential

How you respond to a crisis or a challenge is essential, Mike explains: "You always have a choice. You can choose to turn your back on the world or you can decide to move forward and make the best of the future. It doesn't matter whether you're dealing with bankruptcy, divorce, or a spinal cord injury. The potential for a better future is there, depending on your attitude."

Mike uses the inspiring example of actor Christopher Reeve, who was severely injured in a riding accident but went on to become an activist for the disabled. Thanks, in part, to his actions, the US has passed specific legislation on behalf of America's disabled community.

Beckie feels that Mike's strong values helped him greatly through the rehabilitation process. "Mike always knew his path," she says. "So when he came to a crossroads, it was always very clear what he had to do. There was no way he was going to give up."

And yet Mike claims that his own resolve paled in comparison to others'. "I think what touched me most was the terrible pain that I saw around me while I was going through rehab," says Mike. "There were huge numbers of people who were managing to cope in spite of genuine agony. It just showed me what the human spirit is capable of. People like Helen, Dave, and my roommate, Bob, were a continual inspiration. It moved me over and over again to see so many others getting on with their own Plan B."

"I'm a very optimistic person and I've usually managed to conquer adversity," he adds. "But not on the scale that I was able to see around me. The image of that kind of resilience has really stayed with me. I continue to be inspired by it."

LESSON FIVE:
The Acute Health Care System Worked for Me

"You don't hear people praising the health care system nearly enough," says Mike. "There are many concerns that need to be addressed when it comes to things like patient waiting lists, but we also have many things to be thankful for. G. F. Strong is one of the top four spinal-cord rehab facilities in the world. And I was operated on by Dr. Marcel Dvorak, who's one of the top spinal surgeons in the world as well.

"All the health care professionals I met as a result of my accident were also first-rate, whether you're talking about Maura Whittaker, Rob Giachino, or the many support staff who helped me though my injury."

LESSON SIX:
The Wisdom of Alternative Medicine

"I feel that we need to find a better way to combine the benefits of alternative Eastern medicine with the acute care approach of the West," Mike comments. "Alternative approaches like acupuncture and chi-gong really helped me on the road to wellness.

"There are huge strengths to the Western acute care system," he adds. "But there's other things we can learn in terms of dealing with pain and wellness. The West has a long way to go yet. We could have a really good health care system if we put more emphasis on how we can learn from the best of [the] East and West. There's a lot of wisdom in some of these Eastern approaches, so let's be open and learn."

LESSON SEVEN:
The Barriers of the Spinal Cord World

"I learned a lot about the barriers that people face after a spinal cord injury," says Mike. "The high rate of unemployment, lack of services, and transportation challenges that tie into the whole idea of accessibility. Learning about these challenges in a personal way not only enriched my knowledge of accessibility but it also led to my work with Rick Hansen, ICORD, and issues of accessibility for the disabled."

LESSON EIGHT:
The Need to Stay Engaged

"Making things happen is the basis of being a good citizen," Mike says. He adds: "I'm very impatient with young people who say, 'Well, I'm too good for politics.' Or 'It's too boring—it doesn't amuse me.' It's as though they're a consumer that you've got to sell on the concept of good citizenship.

"If you're not happy about things, go create your own party and make changes," he says. "You're not a consumer that we should have to entice into voting. One of your responsibilities is to be active and engaged."

Mike believes that politics often get unfairly maligned, both by the public and the media. One of his favourite scenes from a movie appears in Monty

Python's *The Life of Brian*, where a character played by John Cleese tries to incite a revolt against the Romans. When he asks what the Romans have done for the public good, the initially timid crowd rebukes him thus, "Apart from the sanitation, education, medicine, wine, public order, irrigation, roads, the fresh water system and public health, what have the Romans ever done for us?"

Mike doesn't want others to forget all the good that can come from public service. He believes especially in the benefits of volunteering. "The reason that our system works is that we have people who go out and do things like coach kids' sports teams, donate their time to cultural organizations, or volunteer with conservation groups," he says. "It's really an essential part of contributing to our society.

"Being active in my community has added so much to my life," Mike explains, adding, "and the opportunity to stay active continues to make every day worthwhile."

LESSON NINE:
Use Your Experiences for Personal Growth

"After the accident, I became so much more committed to the issues of the disabled in a way that I would have never imagined when I was going through Plan A," says Mike. "It was seeing things in a kind of awful and difficult way, but it was also very intimate, and that intimacy really helped add meaning to getting on with Plan B."

LESSON TEN:
The Importance of Love, Family, and Friends

"The importance of love has been reaffirmed tremendously by the experience that I've had," says Mike. "I'm not a traditionally religious person, but I've been struck by the fact that there are spiritual values which are hugely important. I've never taken them for granted, but now I just feel them very profoundly."

As Beckie explains, they've begun to find a renewed sense of what works for them as a couple. Their recent experience has reaffirmed the value of making time for friends and loved ones. "We've always strived to find a true balance in life," she says. "There have been many years, especially the political years, when that really wasn't entirely possible. But both of us really feel that we're getting there."

∽∼∾

One of Mike's favourite stories is the aboriginal tale of *The Dream Catcher*. He likes the idea that dreams can float by and that life gives you opportunities to catch them. "Life is full of people like that," he says. "People who chase their dreams and catch them."

For Mike, the cottage on North Pender Island is where a lot of his dreams seem to have gathered overhead. Together, Beckie and Mike return regularly to the cottage and get as much enjoyment out of it as always. Mike jokes that there is an extra thick railing around the patio and a new cedar fence beyond that. "Not even I could get through all that," he jokes.

For Beckie and Mike, the countless fond memories that surround Pender will always outweigh that terrible day in November. "From that little property, you get a sense of all the issues that are really important to me," says Mike. "Whether it's land and resource management, aboriginal issues, or protecting our environmental breathing space—or the joy of being with family and friends—it's all there in microcosm."

Mike Harcourt has been through a great deal, but there's much left to do. "I'm still a work in progress," he says. "There's lots more to accomplish. Maybe that's why I'm still around."

Today, Mike and Beckie walk along the paths of Pender and islanders roll down the windows of their cars to greet him and shout words of encouragement. Mike always gives a big wave back. If the soft light happens to be right on a lazy Pender afternoon, it's almost as if he's reaching for another dream.

INDEX